U2

U2

A Musical Biography

David Kootnikoff

THE STORY OF THE BAND
CHRIS SMITH, SERIES EDITOR

GREENWOOD PRESS

An Imprint of ABC-CLIO, LLC

A B C C L I O

Santa Barbara, California • Denver, Colorado • Oxford, England

11/10

Copyright 2010 by David Kootnikoff

All rights reserved. No part of this publication may be reproduced, stored in a retrieval system, or transmitted, in any form or by any means, electronic, mechanical, photocopying, recording, or otherwise, except for the inclusion of brief quotations in a review, without prior permission in writing from the publisher.

Library of Congress Cataloging-in-Publication Data

Kootnikoff, David.
  U2: a musical biography / David Kootnikoff.
    p. cm. — (The story of the band)
  Includes index.
    ISBN 978-0-313-36523-2 (alk. paper) — ISBN 978-0-313-36524-9 (ebook) 1. U2 (Musical group) 2. Rock musicians—Ireland—Biography. I. Title.
  ML421.U2K6 2010
  782.42166092'2—dc22
  [B]   2009046477

14 13 12 11 10   1 2 3 4 5

This book is also available on the World Wide Web as an eBook.

Visit www.abc-clio.com for details.

Greenwood Press
An Imprint of ABC-CLIO, LLC

ABC-CLIO, LLC
130 Cremona Drive, P.O. Box 1911
Santa Barbara, California 93116-1911

This book is printed on acid-free paper ∞

Manufactured in the United States of America

For Yuko—The Sweetest Thing

"On earth as it is in heaven"
Matthew 6:10

Contents

Photo essay follows page 88

Series Foreword

Green Day! The Beatles! U2! The Rolling Stones! These are just a few of the many bands that have shaped our lives. Written for high school students and general readers, each volume in this exciting series traces the life of a band from its beginning to the present day. Each examines the early life and family of band members, their formative years, their inspirations, their career preparation and training, and the band's awards, achievements, and lasting contributions to music.

Designed to foster student research, the series has a convenient format. Each book begins with a timeline that charts the major events in the life of the band. The narrative chapters that follow trace the birth, growth, and lasting influence of the band across time. Appendices highlight awards and other accomplishments, and a selected bibliography lists the most important print and electronic resources for high school student research—or for anyone just interested in learning more about the band.

These books also help students learn about social history. Music, perhaps more than any other force, has shaped our culture, especially in recent times. Songs comment on the events of their era and capture the spirit of their age. They powerfully touch the lives of listeners and help people—especially young people—define who they are. So, too, the lifestyles of band members reflect larger social trends and promote and provoke reactions within society. By learning about the bands, students also learn more about the world they live in.

So have a seat, settle in, and crank up the volume!

Introduction

No band in the universe is as big as U2: as the joke goes, when Bono wants to change a light bulb, all he has to do is hold it and the world revolves around him. Few bands have blurred the line between rapture and corn quite like the Sonic Leprechaun and his Irish Soul Men. Yet at their best, U2 achieve what very few artists in any genre can: they create work with a sustained intensity that can transform the particular into the universal. As Bono has said, "A song can change the world . . . it can change the temperature in the room." Listening to U2 can often be a transformative experience, cathartic and exhilarating.

How do they do it? For almost 30 years, U2 has been reaching for the heights and creating music that is as intense and powerful as it is uplifting. Rising from the detritus of punk in the late 1970s, they displayed in their early days an ambition that often belied their combined talents. But they persevered, playing in the discos and pubs around Dublin until their craft began to match the soul-splitting panorama of their ambitions. The remarkable component of their story is how from the very early days they believed in what they were doing. U2 was never only a side project or a diversion. What sets all great bands apart is an uncompromising faith in their own mission, and U2 has always had it.

No band can rise to its heights without attracting some amount of scorn or criticism. U2 has been accused of grandstanding, of placing power before passion, and of putting politics before the music. In the past decade Bono's commitment to Africa and to eradicating poverty has threatened to overwhelm U2. Some people—no less a figure than Larry Mullen Jr., in fact—have accused him of gallivanting around with war criminals when he was seen with political leaders such as President George W. Bush and Prime Minister Tony Blair. Moreover, some critics charge that his zealous support of African causes has perpetuated the neo-colonialism that frames Western powers as saviors of the continent while encouraging the view that Africans are unable to help themselves.

It is one thing to achieve success, but another to sustain it for as long as U2 has. The band's secret resides in their ability to harness the power that lies at the heart of the contradicting forces of faith and doubt, love and hate, life and death. The story of U2 is the grace of discovering we are one while at the same time realizing we are not the same.

Timeline

March 13, 1960	Adam Clayton is born at his grandparents' house in Chinnor in Oxfordshire, England.
May 10, 1960	Paul "Bono" Hewson is born at the Rotunda Hospital in Dublin, Ireland, to Bob and Iris Hewson.
August 8, 1961	David "The Edge" Evans is born in Barking Maternity Hospital in East London to Garvin and Gwenda Evans.
October 31, 1960	Larry Mullen Jr. is born in Dublin to Larry Sr. and Maureen Mullen.
1972	Mount Temple School is established in Dublin, and one of its first students is Paul Hewson.
1973	Paul Hewson and Derek "Guggi" Rowen meet Fionan "Gavin Friday" Hanvey.
	Dave Evans enters Mount Temple.
1974	Larry Mullen Jr. enters Mount Temple.
September 12, 1974	Paul's mother, Iris Hewson, dies from a brain hemorrhage.

1976	Paul and his friends form Lypton Village. Paul becomes "Bonavox of O'Connell Street," then "Bono Vox," and finally "Bono."
Summer 1976	Adam spends a month in Pakistan. He starts to smoke hash.
September 1976	Adam enters Mount Temple.
September 25, 1976	The current members of U2 meet in Larry's kitchen for the first time after responding to a note Larry posted at school about starting a band. They decide to call themselves Feedback.
Autumn/ Winter 1976–77	Feedback plays its first performance in the Mount Temple cafeteria.
April 11, 1977	Feedback plays its first show in front of a paying audience at St. Fintan's School, Dublin. Shortly after, the band decides to change their name to The Hype.
June 1977	The first issue of *Hot Press* music magazine appears.
October 21, 1977	The Hype attends the Clash concert at Trinity College in Dublin and is blown away.
February/March 1978	The Hype plays its first RTE broadcast on the program *Our Times*. The band changes their name to U2.
March 1978	Adam is kicked out of Mount Temple after running naked through the halls.
March 18, 1978	U2 wins the St. Patrick's Day contest in Limerick. The prize is £500 and a demo session with CBS Ireland.
March 30, 1978	U2 gets their first mention in *Hot Press*.
April 1978	U2 meets *Hot Press* journalist Bill Graham. U2 records its first demo at Keystone Studios.
May 25, 1978	U2 meets Paul McGuinness, who soon after becomes their manager.

August 16, 1978	On a family trip to New York, Edge buys a used Gibson Explorer guitar.
September 23, 1978	U2 meets future soundman Joe O'Herlihy while playing the Arcadia Ballroom in Cork.
October 1978	U2 plays the benefit "Rock Against Sexism" at the Magnet Bar in Dublin.
November 1978	Larry's mother is killed in a car accident in Dublin.
April 1979	Bono and Ali travel to London to promote the band.
May 1979	U2 plays the first of six Dandelion Market gigs.
June 1979	U2 signs a contract with CBS Ireland.
September 1979	U2 releases three-song EP *Boy/Girl*; 1,000 copies sell out almost immediately.
October 1979	U2 appears on the cover of *Hot Press* for the first time.
November 10, 1979	U2 appears on the cover of *Record Mirror*.
December 1979	U2 embarks on its first tour of England.
January 15, 1980	U2 plays *The Late Show* for the first time.
March 23, 1980	U2 signs its first international contract with Island Records.
April 5–6, 1980	U2 records "11 O'clock Tick Tock" with Martin Hannett in Dublin's Windmill Lane Studios.
May 23, 1980	U2's first international single, "11 O'clock Tick Tock," is released.
July 1980	U2 begins recording its first album, *Boy*, with Steve Lillywhite.
July 27, 1980	U2 plays its first open-air concert at Leixlip Castle in front of 15,000.
August 1980	U2 releases its first Steve Lillywhite single, "A Day without Me."

October 20, 1980	*Boy* is released and eventually peaks at number 52 in the British charts.
December 3, 1980	U2 plays its first show in France at the Baltard Pavilion in Paris.
December 4, 1980	U2 flies to the US.
December 6, 1980	U2 plays its first U.S. concert at the Ritz in New York City.
December 9, 1980	U2 plays its first show in Canada at the El Mocambo in Toronto.
February 1981	U2 receives first mention in *Rolling Stone* magazine, "Here Come The Next Big Thing" by James Henke.
March 3, 1981	*Boy* is released in North America with new cover and reaches number 94 on the charts.
March 22, 1981	Bono leaves his lyric book backstage at a show in Portland.
June 8, 1981	U2 plays to 50,000, its largest crowd, at Pinkpop Festival in the Netherlands.
June 9, 1981	Bruce Springsteen and Pete Townshend meet U2 backstage at the Hammersmith Palais concert in London.
July 1981	U2 begins recording *October* at Dublin's Windmill Lane Studios with Steve Lillywhite.
July 1981	New single "Fire" is released, peaking at number 35.
August 1, 1981	MTV debuts in the US.
August 20, 1981	U2 makes debut on *Top of the Pops* performing "Fire."
October 5, 1981	New single "Gloria" is released, peaking at 55 in the UK and 81 in the US.
October 12, 1981	New album *October* is released, peaking at 11 in the UK and 104 in the US.

November 1981	Edge and Bono quit the band briefly and a crisis of faith occurs. After discussions with Paul, the band re-forms with a stronger commitment.
November–December 1981	U.S. tour.
December 1981	U2 records new song "A Celebration" in Dublin.
February 1982	U.S. tour.
February 11, 1982	U2 meets photographer Anton Corbijn in New Orleans.
March 4, 1982	U2 begins a month-long stint opening for the J. Geils Band.
March 22, 1982	New single "A Celebration/Trash, Trampoline, and the Party Girl" is released.
August 8, 1982	U2 begins recording *War* with Steve Lillywhite at Windmill Lane in Dublin.
August 21, 1982	Bono marries Alison Stewart at a ceremony in Raheny, Dublin. They honeymoon at Island Record boss Chris Blackwell's property in Jamaica.
December 1982	One-month tour of Europe.
December 15–16, 1982	Video shoot for "New Year's Day" in Salen, Sweden.
January 1983	New single "New Year's Day" is released, peaking at number 10 in the UK.
February 28, 1983	*War* is released and reaches number 1 in the UK and number 12 in the US.
March 1983	New single "Two Hearts Beat as One" is released.
April 1983	Edge records on Jah Wobble's album *Snake Charmer*.
April 3, 1983	U2 records video for "Two Hearts Beat as One" at Sacré Coeur in Paris.

May 21, 1983	U2 meets with reps from the Chicago Peace Museum and agrees to contribute materials.
May 30, 1983	U2 plays the U.S. Festival.
June 5, 1983	U2 plays Red Rocks Amphitheatre near Denver and films it for a future video release.
July 12, 1983	Edge marries Aislinn O'Sullivan in Enniskerry. They honeymoon in Sri Lanka.
August 1983	Irish Prime Minister Garrett Fitzgerald asks Bono to join the Select Government Action Committee on Unemployment.
November 21, 1983	*U2 Live—Under a Blood Red Sky,* produced by Jimmy Iovine, is released, peaking at number 2 in the UK and 28 in the US.
November 22, 1983	U2 plays their first show in Osaka, Japan.
March 1984	Adam is arrested in Dublin for dangerous and drunk driving.
May 1984	*U2 Live at Red Rocks—Under a Blood Red Sky* video is released.
May 7, 1984	U2 begins work on *The Unforgettable Fire* at Slane Castle with Brian Eno and Daniel Lanois.
July 8, 1984	Bono interviews Bob Dylan for *Hot Press* and joins him onstage at a Slane Castle concert.
August 1984	U2 films video for "Pride (In the Name of Love)."
August 1, 1984	U2 launches their own label, Mother Records.
August 29, 1984	U2 plays their first show in Christchurch, New Zealand.
September 1, 1984	U2 meets Greg Carroll and offers him a job.
September 4, 1984	U2 plays their first show in Sydney, Australia.
October 1, 1984	U2 releases its fourth studio album, *The Unforgettable Fire,* peaking at number 1 in the UK and 12 in the US.

November 25, 1984	Bono and Adam participate in the Band Aid recording of the charity single "Do They Know It's Christmas?"
March 14, 1985	*Rolling Stone* puts U2 on its cover with the caption, "Our Choice: Band of the 80s."
May 1985	U2 releases four-track EP *Wide Awake in America,* peaking at number 11 in the UK and 37 in the US.
June 29, 1985	U2 plays homecoming show at Croke Park, Dublin, for 57,000 fans.
July 13, 1985	U2 plays Live Aid at Wembley Stadium in London for estimated audience of 1.5 billion TV viewers.
September 1985	Bono and Ali fly to Ajibar, Ethiopia, to do relief work.
October 1985	Bono flies to New York to participate in Artists United against Apartheid project "Sun City." Meets the Rolling Stones and records "Silver and Gold" with Ron Wood and Keith Richards.
January 1986	U2 begins work on *The Joshua Tree* in Danesmoate House in the south of Dublin with Eno and Lanois. Irish band Clannad releases "In a Lifetime" with Bono on vocals.
April 1986	Larry plays on Paul Brady's album, *Back to the Centre.*
May 17, 1986	U2 headlines *Self Aid* benefit for the unemployed in Dublin.
June 4, 1986	Amnesty International's *Conspiracy of Hope* tour opens in San Francisco.
July 3, 1986	Greg Carroll dies in a motorcycle accident in Dublin.
July 10, 1986	Bono, Ali, and Larry attend Greg's funeral in New Zealand.

July 1986	Bono and Ali visit Nicaragua and El Salvador with Central American Mission Partners.
September 1986	Edge's soundtrack, *Captive*, is released in the UK.
December 14–16, 1986	U2 spends three days in the California desert with Anton Corbijn shooting photos for the new album.
March 4, 1987	New single "With or Without You" is released, peaking at number 1 in the US and number 4 in the UK.
March 9, 1987	U2 releases *The Joshua Tree*, peaking at number 1 in both the UK and US.
March 16, 1987	U2 appears on *The Late Show* for a Dubliners' tribute performing "Springhill Mining Disaster."
April 2, 1987	*The Joshua Tree* tour opens in Tempe, Arizona.
April 6, 1987	U2 meets Frank Sinatra at the Golden Nugget in Las Vegas.
April 27, 1987	U2 appears on the cover of *Time* magazine with caption "U2: Rock's Hottest Ticket."
May 1987	New single "I Still Haven't Found What I'm Looking For" is released, peaking at number 1 in the US and 6 in the UK.
May 13, 1987	*The Joshua Tree* is certified Multi-Platinum by RIAA.
June 2, 1987	U2 meets Roy Orbison at Wembley Arena in London.
August 1987	New single "Where The Streets Have No Name" is released, peaking at number 4 in the UK and 13 in the US.
September 1987	Director Phil Joanou is confirmed as director of upcoming film *Rattle and Hum*.
September 26, 1987	U2 visits Greater Calvary Baptist Church and meets New Voices of Freedom gospel choir. The event is captured on film by Joanou.

October 12, 1987	U2 appears on the Special Olympics charity album *A Very Special Christmas* covering "Christmas (Baby, Please Come Home)."
November 8, 1987	Joanou captures U2's performance at McNichols Sports Arena in Denver on film.
November 11, 1987	U2 plays free outdoor "Save the Yuppies" concert at Herman Plaza in San Francisco.
November 29, 1987	U2 records "Angel of Harlem," "When Love Comes to Town," and others at Sun Studios in Memphis.
December 20, 1987	*The Joshua Tree* tour wraps up in Tempe, Arizona.
March 2, 1988	*The Joshua Tree* wins two Grammys: Album of the Year and Best Rock Duo or Group with Vocal
May 1988	Phil Joanou records the band performing "Desire" in Dublin.
June 1988	U2 moves to LA to finish work on the *Rattle and Hum* soundtrack.
September 1988	U2 appears on the Woody Guthrie/Leadbelly tribute album *Folkways: A Vision Shared* performing "Jesus Christ."
September 19, 1988	New single "Desire" is released, peaking at number 1 in the UK and 3 in the US.
October 10–11, 1988	*Rattle and Hum* album is released, peaking at number 1 in the US, UK, Australia, and Canada among other countries.
November 4, 1988	*Rattle and Hum* film opens around the world.
December 8, 1988	New single "Angel of Harlem" is released, peaking at number 9 in the UK and 14 in the US.
January 17, 1989	*Rattle and Hum* is certified Multi-Platinum.
February 1, 1989	Roy Orbison's *Mystery Girl* album is released containing Bono and Edge's "She's a Mystery to Me."

March 6, 1989	Edge travels to Moscow to support Greenpeace benefit album.
April 1989	New single "When Love Comes to Town" is released, peaking at number 6 in the UK and 68 in the US.
August 6, 1989	Adam is charged with possession of marijuana.
December 27–30, 1989	U2 wraps up the decade with a series of shows at Point Depot in Dublin.
January 17, 1990	Bono inducts the Who into the Rock and Roll Hall of Fame.
February 6, 1990	*A Clockwork Orange 2004* debuts in London with music by Bono and Edge.
October 1990	U2 covers Cole Porter's "Night and Day" for the *Red Hot and Blue* compilation.
October 3, 1990	U2 travels to Berlin to begin work on *Achtung Baby* with Daniel Lanois.
January 1991	U2 returns to Dublin to finish work on the album.
March 1991	Edge and wife Aislinn separate.
September 1991	U2 shoots video for "The Fly" in Dublin and London.
September 5, 1991	Island Records sues SST Records and Negativland for their single "U2."
October 1991	U2 shoots video for "Mysterious Ways" in Fez, Morocco.
October 21–22, 1991	New single "The Fly" is released, peaking at number 1 in the UK and 61 in the US.
November 18–19, 1991	*Achtung Baby* is released peaking at number 2 in the UK and 1 in the US.
November 24–25, 1991	New single "Mysterious Ways" is released, peaking at number 9 in the US and 13 in the UK.
January 15, 1992	Edge inducts the Yardbirds into the Rock and Roll Hall of Fame.

February 29, 1992	*Zoo TV* tour opens in Lakeland, Florida.
March 1992	New single "One" is released, peaking at number 7 in the UK and 10 in the US. U2 donates royalties to AIDS research.
June 7–8, 1992	New single "Even Better Than the Real Thing" is released, peaking at 12 in the UK and 32 in the US.
June 20, 1992	U2 participates in a Greenpeace protest at Sellafield nuclear plant.
September 14, 1992	U2 meets presidential candidate Bill Clinton at Chicago's Ritz Carlton Hotel.
December 1992	Bono appears on the cover of British *Vogue* with Christy Turlington.
January 20, 1993	Larry and Adam attend the inauguration of President Bill Clinton.
May 1, 1993	Adam and Naomi Campbell announce their engagement.
May 9, 1993	*Zooropa* tour kicks off in Rotterdam.
June 1993	U2 releases "Numb" as a video single.
June 2, 1993	U2 and Island Records announce an extension the band's current contract, making U2 the highest paid act in rock history.
July 5–6, 1993	U2 releases *Zooropa*, peaking at number 1 in the US and UK.
July 17, 1993	U2 begins including live feed broadcasts from Sarajevo into their shows.
August 11, 1993	Salman Rushdie joins U2 onstage at Wembley Stadium in London.
September 1993	New single "Lemon" appears in limited release.
November 5, 1993	Bono shoots video of "I've Got You Under My Skin" with Frank Sinatra in Palm Springs, California.

November 22–23, 1993	New single "Stay (Faraway, So Close)" is released, peaking at number 4 in the UK and US.
November 26, 1993	Adam goes on a drinking binge and misses a concert in Sydney, Australia. Bass technician Stuart Morgan fills in.
December 10, 1993	U2 plays last show of *Zoo TV/Zooropa/Zoomerang* tours in Tokyo, Japan.
January 19, 1994	Bono inducts Bob Marley into Rock and Roll Hall of Fame.
January 25, 1994	*In the Name of the Father* soundtrack is released. Bono cowrote the title track and "You Made Me the Thief of Your Heart."
March 1, 1994	Bono introduces Frank Sinatra at the Grammys. U2 picks up a Grammy for Best Alternative Album, *Zooropa*.
May 25, 1994	U2 earns the Ivor Novello Award for International Achievement.
September 13, 1994	Larry and Adam appear on Nanci Griffiths' *Flyer* album, released on this day.
January 1995	*Melon: Remixes for Propaganda* is released to fan club members.
June 5–6, 1995	New single "Hold Me, Thrill Me, Kiss Me, Kill Me" is released, peaking at number 2 in the UK and 16 in the US.
September 12, 1995	Bono, Edge, and Brian Eno perform "Miss Sarajevo" and "One" at Luciano Pavarotti's charity concert in Modena, Italy.
September 26, 1995	Bono's version of "Hallelujah" appears on *Tower of Song: The Songs of Leonard Cohen*.
November 6–7, 1995	*Original Soundtracks 1* by Passengers, a collaboration between Brian Eno and U2, is released.
December 30, 1995	Bono and Ali fly to Sarajevo for the New Year.

May 11, 1996	Bill Graham, the Irish rock journalist and old friend of U2, dies.
May 14, 1996	*Mission Impossible* soundtrack is released. Larry and Adam play on the title track.
February 3–4, 1997	New single "Discotheque" is released, peaking at number 1 in the UK and number 10 in the US.
March 3–4, 1997	*Pop* is released, debuting at number 1 in more than 30 countries.
April 14–15, 1997	New single "Staring at the Sun" is released, peaking at number 3 in the UK and 26 in the US.
April 25, 1997	U2 opens *PopMart* tour in Las Vegas.
July 14–15, 1997	New single "Last Night on Earth" is released, peaking at number 10 in the UK and 57 in the US.
August 12, 1997	U2 plays first show in Poland.
September 9, 1997	"I'm Not Your Baby," U2's collaboration with Sinead O'Connor on *The End Of Violence* soundtrack, is released.
September 23, 1997	U2 plays historic show in Sarajevo.
September 30, 1997	U2 plays first show in Israel.
October 20–21, 1997	New single "Please" is released, peaking at number 7 in the UK but failing to chart in the US.
December 2, 1997	U2's security chief is seriously injured in Mexico City when President Ernesto Zedillo's sons try to get into the concert without an invitation.
December 12, 1997	U2 plays its last U.S. PopMart show in Seattle.
January 27, 1998	U2 plays Rio de Janeiro, their first South American show.
March 16–21, 1998	U2 plays its first concerts in South Africa and wraps up its 11-month PopMart tour.

May 19, 1998	U2 performs in Belfast in support of the Yes campaign for the Irish Peace Agreement.
September 29, 1998	Bono sings on Kris Franklin's "Lean on Me" from *The Nu Nation Project*.
October 19–20, 1998	A new version of "The Sweetest Thing" is released, peaking at number 3 in the UK and 63 in the US despite not having a commercial release.
November 2–3, 1998	U2 releases its first retrospective, *U2 The Best of 1980–1990,* peaking at number 1 in the UK and 2 in the US.
February 16, 1999	Bono helps launch Jubilee 2000 campaign.
March 15, 1999	Bono inducts Bruce Springsteen into the Rock and Roll Hall of Fame.
September 14, 1999	Bono's collaboration with Wyclef Jean, "New Day," is released.
September 23, 1999	Bono joins Bob Geldof and other members of Jubilee 2000 to visit Pope John Paul II in the Alban Hills outside of Rome.
October 9, 1999	Bono helps launch charity concert NetAid at Giants Stadium in New Jersey.
February 9, 2000	Bono attend the premiere in Berlin of his film, *The Million Dollar Hotel.*
March 13–14, 2000	*The Million Dollar Hotel* soundtrack is released.
March 18, 2000	U2 and Paul McGuinness receive the Freedom of Dublin.
July 18, 2000	U2.com opens.
September 7, 2000	Bono appears with Nigerian President Olusegun Obasanjo at the UN Millennium Summit to present a petition of more than 21 million signatures calling for debt relief.
October 9–10, 2000	U2 releases new single "Beautiful Day," peaking at number 1 in the UK and 21 in the US despite not having a commercial release.

October 30, 2000	*All That You Can't Leave Behind* is released, debuting at number 1 in 32 countries and number 3 in the US.
January 29, 2001	New single "Stuck in a Moment You Can't Get Out Of" is released in the UK, peaking at number 2.
February 21, 2001	U2 wins three Grammys: Best Rock Group, Song of the Year for "Beautiful Day," Record of the Year for *All That You Can't Leave Behind*.
March 24, 2001	U2 opens *Elevation* tour in Miami.
July 20–21, 2001	Bono attends G8 Summit in Genoa, Italy, with Bob Geldof.
August 21, 2001	Bono's father, Bob Hewson, dies of cancer.
October 10, 2001	U2 opens third leg of *Elevation* tour in South Bend, Indiana.
November 19, 2001	Bono appears on "Joy" from Mick Jagger's solo album *Goddess in the Doorway*.
January 22, 2002	U2 releases EP 7, sold only through Target department stores.
January 31, 2002	Bono attends World Economic Forum in New York.
February 3, 2002	U2 performs at the New Orleans Super Bowl halftime show.
February 24, 2002	Bono is on the cover of *Time* magazine under the caption "Can Bono Save the World?"
February 27, 2002	U2 wins four Grammys: Best Rock Album, Record of the Year for "Walk On," Best Pop song for "Stuck in a Moment You Can't Get Out Of," Best Rock Song for "Elevation."
May 24, 2002	Bono begins an African tour in Ghana with U.S. Treasury Secretary Paul O'Neill.
June 17, 2002	Edge and Morleigh marry in Dublin.

October 21–22, 2002	New single "Electrical Storm" is released, peaking at number 4 in the UK and 77 in the US, where there is no commercial release.
November 4–5, 2002	U2 releases *The Best of 1990–2000*.
November 18, 2002	Bono receives Humanitarian Laureate Award from the Simon Wiesenthal Center.
December 1, 2002	Bono opens *The Heart of America* tour organized by DATA on AIDS Day.
December 17, 2002	New song "The Hands That Built America" appears on the *Gangs of New York* soundtrack.
January 19, 2003	"The Hands That Built America" wins Golden Globe Award for Best Song.
February 21, 2003	Bono is honored as MusiCares 2003 Person of the Year.
October 8, 2003	Bono is one of the featured speakers at the 2003 Global Leadership and Humanitarian Action Awards.
November 29, 2003	Bono and Edge perform at the 46664 concert in Cape Town, South Africa, to raise funds to fight AIDS in Africa.
January 17, 2004	Bono is honored for his humanitarian efforts by the King Center in Atlanta.
March 25, 2004	*Rolling Stone* features U2 on its cover as one of its "immortals" of rock.
April 18, 2004	*Time* lists Bono as one its 100 most influential people.
May 16, 2004	Bono helps launch DATA's ONE Campaign.
November 22–23, 2004	*How to Dismantle an Atomic Bomb* is released, debuting at number 1 in the UK and US.
February 13, 2005	U2 wins three Grammys: Best Video, Best Song, and Best Rock Performance for "Vertigo."

March 14, 2005	Bruce Springsteen inducts U2 into the Rock and Roll Hall of Fame.
March 26, 2005	*Vertigo* tour opens in Los Angeles.
July 2, 2005	U2 opens Live 8 with Paul McCartney.
December 10, 2005	Amnesty International honors U2 with its 2005 Ambassadors of Conscience award.
December 18, 2005	*Time* names Bono and Bill and Melinda Gates as their Persons of the Year.
January 25, 2006	Bono attends World Economic Forum in Davos, Switzerland.
February 8, 2006	U2 wins five Grammys: Album of the Year, Song of the Year for "Sometimes You Can't Make It on Your Own," Best Rock Song for "City of Blinding Lights," Best Rock Album, and Best Rock Group.
February 12, 2006	U2 opens fourth leg of *Vertigo* tour in Monterrey, Mexico.
May 16, 2006	Bono edits the *Independent* newspaper.
June 16, 2006	Edge unveils a sculpture in Dublin dedicated to Rory Gallagher.
August 29, 2006	*Rogue's Gallery* is released with Bono's version of "A Dying Sailor to His Shipmates."
September 22, 2006	The book *U2 by U2* is released.
September 25, 2006	U2 and Green Day perform a set before a Monday Night Football Game at the Superdome in New Orleans.
November 6, 2006	"The Saints Are Coming" is released.
November 7, 2006	*Vertigo* tour kicks off in Brisbane, Australia.
January 1, 2007	"Window in the Skies" is released.
March 1, 2007	Bono is honored by the NAACP in Los Angeles.

March 29, 2007	Bono receives honorary British knighthood in Dublin.
May 20, 2007	U2 3D is screened at Cannes.
September 27, 2007	Bono and DATA are honored with Liberty Medal in Philadelphia and he speaks out against torture.
November 2007	Remastered *The Joshua Tree* is released.
June 2008	U2's first three albums—*Boy, October, War*—are re-released.
August 2008	Portions of the new album leak on the Internet.
January 2009	U2 performs at the *We Are One* concert held for the inauguration of newly elected President Barack Obama.
February 16, 2009	New single "Get on Your Boots" is released, peaking at number 12 in the UK and 40 in the US.
February 27, 2009	U2's twelfth studio album, *No Line on the Horizon,* is released, peaking at number 1 in the UK and the US.
March 2009	Paul announces U2 *360°* stadium tour will begin in the fall of 2009.
	In an issue of *Rolling Stone*, Bono announces that a new album, *Songs of Ascent,* will be released in 2010.

CHAPTER ONE

Stories for Boys: Origins & Early Days (1976–1980)

In the middle of the 1970s, Dublin was suffering from the same malaise that was burning up London and New York. The Eagles and Peter Frampton were filling the airwaves with middle-of-the-road dirges more reminiscent of a Sunday hangover than a Saturday-night party. The underground was bubbling up and punk was about to break through, but Ireland was still a musical backwater. Everyone looked to London, which looked to New York or Berlin, for cues. The only significant musical offerings Dublin had made in the last twenty years were folk stars the Dubliners and heavy-metal warriors Thin Lizzy. Change was long overdue.

On the northern outskirts of Dublin, a group of teenagers that would later transform the world with the sheer force of their collective will and dedication to an original vision were lazily kicking around a schoolyard, searching for adventure. The four boys that would eventually form U2 were fifteen and sixteen in 1976. They were all enrolled in Mount Temple, a comprehensive school that accepted children from both Protestant and Catholic backgrounds. It was the first ever non-denominational school in Ireland and was a unique experiment for the time, part idealism and part pragmatism. Dublin's rising middle-class was increasingly caring less for religious divisions and more about getting on in the world. The future members of U2 came from both denominations, and it's unlikely they would have met anywhere else.

Adam Clayton was the oldest and most eccentric of the bunch. He played bass guitar, grew his hair into a blonde afro and wore an afghan coat. He was born in England on March 13, 1960 in the village of Chinnor outside of Oxford, where his father worked as a pilot for British Airways. The family had lived in Nairobi, Kenya, until 1965 before settling in Malahide, just outside of Dublin. Adam briefly attended St. Andrews Church of Ireland School and had a hard time fitting into the boarding school of St. Columba's until his grades got so bad his parents pulled him out. While at school, he earned a reputation for being slightly off-center, but was always very polite to everyone. He'd bring a thermos into class and help himself to a cup of coffee during lessons, and was never too concerned about what others thought of him.

Paul Hewson was restless and looking for some excitement. Born May 10, 1960, he was a mischievous and rambunctious child who earned the family nickname "the antichrist"[1] for all the disturbances he caused around the house. There was music in his home, and his father, Bob Hewson, was a huge opera fan. Paul took to playing chess and became quite good. He also learned some guitar, sang, and rebelled against the loneliness of his home life. His mother, Iris, had died from a brain hemorrhage when he was fourteen, and he was living with his dad and older brother, Norman. He missed her immensely and was searching for answers. He would eventually adopt the name Bono Vox, cockeyed Latin for "good voice," and spend more and more time away from his home. He recalls:

> My mother's death just threw petrol on the fire. The big questions just built to a crescendo. I felt hopeless. I thought about suicide. I was thinking too hard about everything.[2]

He began discussing his problems with a teacher of religion at school and found comfort in her explanations. He started to pray and read the Bible, hooking up with what was to become known as the "Charismatic" movement that included Catholics and Protestants worshipping together throughout Ireland.

Dave Evans was always into gadgets. Together with his older brother, Dick, they built their own electric guitar after his mother had bought his first—a Spanish guitar—when he was only seven. Music was always a big thing around his home, with the Beatles being an early favorite. He was born August 8, 1961, to Welsh parents in Barking, England, just outside of London. In 1962 the family moved to Malahide in the north of Dublin after his father got a promotion at Plessey Engineering. Dave used to get teased for looking like Alfred E. Newman from *MAD* magazine with his freckles, big ears, and overbite. Bono eventually dubbed him "The Edge" for the shape of his head and because he was attracted to edges, both physical and mental, and preferred looking in on things from the outside.[3] At Mount Temple, Edge bumped into Bono, who was a year older. He knew Bono played guitar, but thought he was better. Edge had met Adam when they were seven at St. Andrew's school, but they didn't get to know each other until they met years later at the fateful meeting in Larry Mullen Jr.'s kitchen.

Larry Mullen Jr. had been playing drums since he was nine. Born October 31, 1961, he was in the same year at Mount Temple as Edge, but was over a year younger than Bono and Adam. In 1975 he joined the prestigious Artane Boys Band, but quit after only three days over a disagreement about the length of his hair.[4] He then joined the Post Office Workers' Union Band and played all around Dublin and other parts of the country for the next two years. Larry didn't have much interest in school. His father suggested he put up a notice at school to form a band. On September 25, 1976, the band that was to become U2 met in Larry's kitchen in Artane. Larry recalls,

> It was the Larry Mullen band for about ten minutes, so as not to hurt my feelings. It was also my kitchen. Then Bono came in and that was the end of that. He blew any chance I had of being in charge.[5]

Seven students answered the call, but two—Peter Martin and Ivan McCormick—were quickly dropped. Adam brought his bass (an Ibanez copy of a Gibson EB-3) and Dick and Dave brought along homemade guitars they had built themselves. The four members known today as U2, plus Edge's brother, Dick, formed the nucleus of the band. They were raw amateurs and nowhere near ready to play gigs at this point, but they had a desire to be seen and heard. Bono came up with the name Feedback because that seemed like the only sound they could make. Despite their obvious limitations, they were soon able to put together two songs: Peter Frampton's "Show Me the Way"—a favorite of Bono's—and, for a laugh, the Bay City Rollers' "Bye Bye Baby." Their first gig came at the end of 1976 at a talent show in the school cafeteria at Mount Temple. They appeared as a four-piece, as Dick wasn't a student, and pulled it off putting more bravado and noise into their performance than musical prowess. They made a huge impact, and their fellow students were gobsmacked, mainly by Bono's dramatic stage presence. Adam recalls:

> It was all over in a flash . . . but in that ten minutes a world opened up of how things could be. At the time I thought a riot had taken place—and maybe it had.[6]

The band was inspired to get more serious, and started practicing on weekends at Adam's place in Malahide. During Easter 1977 they got a second gig as Feedback at St. Fintan's, another school in north Dublin. Their first paying gig, they were a late addition to the bill that included two other acts, Rat Salad and the Arthur Phybbes Band. They opened the show with a set that included Chuck Berry's "Johnny B. Goode," the Eagles' "Peaceful Easy Feeling," Frampton's "Show Me the Way," and the Moody Blues' "Nights in White Satin," but they had never worked out a way to end the songs. Their performance stretched into forty minutes and included two female singers, with one playing flute on "Nights in White Satin."[7] Bono sang through a guitar amp, which made his already loud voice sound muddy and distorted. Although they got paid, it was less than stellar to say the least. Members of the audience were laughing. Despite the poor performance, they had developed a loyal following and there was no turning back. They dropped the female singers, changed their name to The Hype, and went to work developing a better live show.

A few months later, Bono thought he had graduated from Mount Temple and was starting at University College Dublin when he was told that there had been a mistake. He had failed Irish, so he had to return to repeat a year. He was happy to oblige, as the rest of the band was still at Mount Temple and so was his girlfriend and future wife, Alison Stewart.

During their early rehearsals, Bono stumbled upon his first song—"What's Going On?"—and the band started to play along. No one had heard of Marvin Gaye, so they were convinced they had a totally original song. They performed it live at the Marine Hotel in October and it was a major turning point in the formation of U2. They were realizing how futile it was trying to perfect versions of "Jumpin' Jack Flash" or "Hotel California." It didn't make sense to form a rock band to do cover versions of other bands' songs. It was much easier, and ultimately smarter, to write your own material—that way no one could compare it with anything else.

Punk had already been making waves in London and the United Kingdom, but it still didn't have much presence in Ireland. One exception—the Dublin band The Radiators From Outer Space and their single "Television Screen"—was an early influence on the nascent U2 sound. U2 had heard the Sex Pistols and Buzzcocks' singles; Adam was into Television and The Clash, whereas Edge admired Patti Smith's debut *Horses* and Robert Quine's guitar playing from Richard Hell's band, the Voidoids. On October 21, the Clash's Get Out Of Control tour hit Trinity College in Dublin, and Bono later said it turned his world upside down.[8]

While the rest of the band was beginning to embrace punk, Larry was chafing against much of what he was hearing. He stuck to more mainstream tastes such as Bruce Springsteen and the Eagles and couldn't relate to the fashion or raw anger of bands like the Sex Pistols or The Clash. Then, when he heard The Ramones, he began to change his mind. Here was a band that played melodic, aggressive songs like "Glad to See You Go" and "Beat on the Brat" with energy and humor that he could relate to.

Bono was getting into the burgeoning alternative scene in Dublin and started to experiment with fashion styles modeled on the singers of the day, such as Iggy Pop on the cover of *The Idiot*. He even showed up at school with a safety pin in his cheek until Ali threatened to break up with him. It hadn't really been pierced—he wore it to get a reaction. It disappeared without a word. Bono, like the rest of the band, was moving in all directions and experimenting with new sounds and styles. Around this time he, along with friends Fionan "Gavin Friday" Hanvey and Derek "Guggi" Rowan, invented a private universe called Lypton Village where all the initiates were given special names to represent their true characters. It was a way to avoid the responsibilities of the adult world and remain as simple and innocent for as long as possible. Bono was christened with his new name, "Bono Vox of O'Connell Street," after a hearing aid shop in the center of Dublin. His first Village name was actually Steinheg-vanhuysenolegbangbangbangbang, but that didn't stick.[10]

Bono was playing guitar and singing, and the band was a five piece with Edge's older brother, now spelled Dik, still a member. Bono eventually gave up guitar and concentrated his energies on being a frontman. The band's first couple of serious original songs were called "The Fool" and "Street Missions," a mix of early David

Bowie and bloated stadium rock. In the winter of 1978, they made their first TV appearance on the RTÉ program *Our Times* performing "The Fool."

The band was moving into new territory and had decided to change their name again when they realized they didn't really have much in common with the punk bands they were hearing. U2 was suggested by Steve Averill, the band's future designer and an ex-member of The Radiators after speaking with Adam who admitted liking the name XTC.[11] It was agreed on because no one hated it, it looked good on posters, and was easy to remember. The attitude of punk was something the band had no problem identifying with—the importance of challenging the status quo and doing things for yourself—but the idea of rejecting everything that came before was harder to reconcile. U2 have always been suspicious of doctrines and resisted being boxed in by anything that might limit their natural musical growth. While the Clash were singing "No Elvis, Beatles or the Rolling Stones,"[12] U2 had been playing a cover of "Jumpin' Jack Flash." Much of U2's power has derived from their willingness to remain open and embrace seemingly contradictory forces. They might not have been fully conscious of it at the time, but they were already displaying their iconoclastic spirit by rebelling against punk conformity.

On St. Patrick's Day 1978, the band, minus Dik, drove to Limerick to participate in the Harp Lager Pop Competition and, to their surprise, advanced to the final round. The next day U2 won, earning a trophy, 500 pounds, and a recording session with CBS Ireland. Convinced they had something special, the win was a defining moment, encouraging the band to do whatever it took to make it. The win also earned them their first ever write-up in *Hot Press,* Ireland's premier music magazine:

> Newly-formed Dublin New Wave band U-2 scored a blow for rock 'n' roll when they won the top prize of £500 in a group contest co-sponsored by the *Evening Press* and Harp Lager held recently during the Civic Week in Limerick. That's what you call getting the breaks. . . .[13]

One of the judges that week was Jackie Hayden of CBS Records, who was impressed and arranged their first demo session a few weeks later at Keystone Studios in Dublin. Larry's father showed up while they were in the middle of recording to take him home to study for his exams the next day. None of the band members felt comfortable in the studio and the results were less than desirable.

Soon after the Limerick competition, U2 met the producer of a youth program on Ireland's national TV network RTÉ, called *Youngline*, who was visiting the school's music teacher about having the school choir perform on the show. Bono, ever the consummate salesman, let it be known that the band was also interested in appearing. After they auditioned with a few Ramones' covers, they were booked. On the show they played two originals, "Street Missions" and a song Edge had written, "Life on a Distant Planet."[14] Apart from some lip-syncing problems, the band sounded tight, but there wasn't much punk in their performance. Bono leapt and pranced around in white slacks and feathered hair resembling the glam singer Jobriath, and Larry looked like an outcast from the British rock group Slade. Edge played a long, melodic solo reminiscent of Irish band Horslips, and Adam was the only one who looked anything like a "new waver" as he flogged his rubbery bass lines all over the mix. In fact, U2 was never much of a punk band. Ireland was a very different place from England, and a bunch of kids from one of Dublin's most progressive schools had very little to revolt against.

Around this time, Bono's friends Guggi and Gavin formed a gothic-rock band called the Virgin Prunes. The two were a big influence on Bono, having invented Lypton Village. Edge's brother, Dik, joined the Prunes after leaving U2. He had been an irregular member and never really fit in. Adam had been kicked out of Mount Temple by this time for running naked through the school and was using his free time to "manage" the band by phoning around for gigs and trying to hustle contacts. He took the initiative and even called Phil Lynott from Thin Lizzy to ask for advice, getting him out of bed in the early morning to pick his brain about booking shows. But with all of U2 yet to graduate from high school, they were fighting an uphill battle.

Hot Press began spilling more ink on the band and one writer, Bill Graham, became an early fan. Adam invited Graham to one of their rehearsals, which proved to be a seminal event in U2's history. They impressed Graham and he advised them to get a good manager, passing on the name of friend Paul McGuinness who he knew was looking for a band to manage. Paul was ten years older than the band, English, but educated in Ireland at Trinity College. U2 was playing at the Project

Arts Center soon after in May, and Paul went down to check them out. He was taken by their unique sound and especially by Bono's stage presence. Paul watched Bono scanning the faces in the crowd, making eye contact and eager to engage everyone in the audience. Paul met them afterward and they hit it off. Paul eventually became the fifth member of U2, known affectionately as "The Goose."[15] To this day, Bono likes to say U2 is a band of four, but a corporation of five.[16]

Soon after meeting Paul, everyone graduated from Mount Temple. They were finally free from school, but new domestic pressures arose. Adam's parents were pressuring him to get a "real" job, and Bono's father gave him one year to seal a record deal or move out. Edge's parents were more easygoing, and Larry got a job with Seiscom Delta, an oil company based in Dublin. Due to his job, Larry started missing rehearsals and a few gigs. Guggi stood in for him during some photo shoots and the rest of the band began questioning Larry's commitment and gave some thought to replacing him.[17] They decided to keep him on when he began to show more dedication.

During that summer of 1978, Edge visited New York City with his family and bought a used Gibson Explorer. It was a unique guitar to have at the time with its zigzag shape, and it soon became Edge's trademark. U2 also played their first benefit gig for the Contraception Action Campaign to support the free availability of condoms in Ireland. At the time, condoms were prohibited and were only legalized later that year. U2's participation heralded their practice of putting their music at the service of worthwhile causes that became synonymous with the group in the future.

In August Bill Graham wrote in *Hot Press*:

> U-2 owe no obvious debts to earlier styles. Their songs are uniquely their own, vibrant celebrations that are both direct in impact yet not so simple in style[18]

It was another huge boost to their confidence. U2's music was maturing and they were including more original numbers in their shows like "Out of Control" and "Shadows and Tall Trees" that would eventually end up on their first album. They were creating a sound that reflected what they were hearing around them while consciously avoiding replicating anyone else. This led to a lot of experimentation with some questionable results.

U2 finally bagged their first important gig and played to over 2,500 people at Dun Laoghaire's Top Hat Ballroom in September, supporting The Stranglers. Paul had a wedding to attend and wasn't there to represent the group, so they didn't get a sound check or even dressing rooms. Bono tried to befriend bassist Jean-Jacques Burnel, but Burnel wasn't interested in the young Irish singer. The Stranglers had been around for over five years, predating punk, and seemed years older than U2. Bono got into a heated argument with Burnel over The Stranglers' snobby, unpunk-like attitude. Later, while they were performing, Bono broke into their dressing room and stole a bottle of wine.[19]

Their friends, the Virgin Prunes, were backing them up at many of these early concerts, but Paul wasn't comfortable with the arrangement. By the time U2 took the stage the Prunes had left the audience on a downer. They were a confrontational, Dadaist-inspired band and enjoyed provoking the crowd, at times mocking them with what they called "Art-F***," a simulation of the sexual act on stage.[20] U2 had a very different approach and was committed to creating an uplifting experience for anyone willing to spend money on one of their shows. The two bands eventually went their own ways, but remained friends.

U2 began experiencing some hardships in the latter half of 1978. They weren't making any money and watched bitterly as cover bands were raking in cash. Frustration set in with each other's mistakes and limitations. Fights broke out and ties were strained. Just when things were looking bad, they played a packed house at the Arcadia Ballroom in Cork (in the south of Ireland) and met their future soundman, Joe O'Herlihy. This successful show outside of Dublin picked up their spirits, and it came time to record another demo at Keystone Studios. Paul arranged for Barry Devlin, the bass player and lead singer from the Irish rock band Horslips, to produce it. Horslips were one of the biggest Irish bands of the 1970s, and U2 looked up to them. The demo included "Street Missions," "The Fool," and "Shadows and Tall Trees." Paul sent it all around to A&R reps in London and in the United States, but nothing came of it. U2 had reached a modest level of popularity in Dublin, but they seemed to have hit a plateau and needed a break to get them to the next level.

Shortly after the recording, tragedy struck Larry's family: his mother was killed in a traffic accident. It tested his commitment to the band, but after the mourning period subsided he realized how important music was to him and he quit his day job. The experience focused his priorities, and he was determined to stay with the band as far as they could go. It also brought him closer to Bono and they began talking openly about the Bible, seeking comfort for their shared loss. Soon they joined Edge in attending meetings with a Christian group called Shalom. They had heard of the group through Guggi and were attracted to their communal lifestyle and the members' lack of material desires.[21] It became a refuge where they could talk openly about their spirituality and explore the scriptures free from any formalized religious dogma.

During this emotional turbulence, U2 continued to gig regularly. In December, they got another spot opening for a notorious band at the time called the Greedy Bastards, consisting of Phil Lynott of Thin Lizzy and ex-Sex Pistols Steve Jones and Paul Cook. Jones ended up borrowing Edge's Explorer and he was flattered at first, but then he freaked out when he realized the condition Jones was in. U2 was turned off by the Bastards and thought they were on their way down, awash in booze and drugs. It was another brush with an older band that left U2 second-guessing their place in the punk rock pantheon. U2 was rebelling against the usual sex, drugs, and rock 'n' roll clichés and trying to develop their own creed.

U2 was constantly on the lookout for new innovations that might set them apart from the pack of other young, hungry bands. Bono suggested Edge purchase a Memory Man delay unit for his guitar that he thought sounded like a punk rock symphony in outer space.[22] With Adam's distinctive bass playing, Edge started experimenting with chord formations that eventually evolved into a richer and more complex sound. He was forming chords with only two notes instead of three, leaving the songs open so that the band could fill in the spaces with fresh rhythms and melodies. Making use of harmonics, Edge began to explore different rhythms to give the music more texture. Bono wanted to keep things fluid and spontaneous, pushing the band to improvise and change directions in the middle of a song. He would often direct the band onstage with a wave of his left hand.

After their last demo failed to generate any label interest, U2 went back into the studio in February 1979 to record some more original songs at a small studio in Dublin. The band was struggling to find their own sound and successful gigs were hit or miss. Label reps would come over from London, as did famed DJ John Peel, but the band never received an offer or any significant attention from the United Kingdom. They were getting impatient, especially Bono, who wanted to go to London to stir up some attention in person. Paul tried to discourage him, but he went anyway in April, taking Ali. For a week they went around to music magazines like *Sounds*, *New Music Express*, and *Record Mirror*, flogging U2's demo and drumming up interest.

In May, U2 landed a gig every Saturday for six weeks at Dublin's Dandelion Market. Their fan base was growing and so was their image. Bono was taking basic theatrical lessons from Mannix Flynn, an actor and writer, and the Dandelion shows helped solidify the band's stagecraft, which marked a turning point in U2's development.[23] Paul was able to convince a couple of CBS reps from London to come to Dublin in June to hear U2's gig at McGonagle's pub and finance a three-song demo. They recorded it in Keystone Studios again with Chas de Whalley from CBS and mixed it at Windmill Studios, but they were disappointed with the results. At one point the head of CBS A&R suggested they drop Larry because he sounded so awful on the demo. The band told him to stuff it.

To promote the new songs the band took turns going on Dave Fanning's radio show, a popular program that showcased local bands. Bono resisted any comparisons to other Irish bands like the Undertones, saying U2's music was "something to hold onto" and hoped no one would squeeze the band into any particular category.[24] The fans were asked to call in and choose what song should become the A-side from the three tracks—"Out of Control," "Stories for Boys," and "Boy/Girl." "Out of Control" won and the *U23 EP* was released in September. Only one thousand copies were pressed, each one manually numbered by Jackie Hayden at CBS Records, and they sold out within days.

Now that they could hear their songs on the radio, the band felt like they were the real thing, and their families took them more seriously. But while London-based *Sounds* magazine did a feature titled "Coming Up For Eire" in September, other factors were pulling in other directions. Edge's parents were pressuring him to enroll in college. He had made a promise with his parents that if the band didn't have a record deal after a year he'd enroll in a natural science course at Kevin Street Technical College. He reluctantly attended, but his dedication to the band never waned.

U2 appeared on the front cover of *Hot Press* for the first time in October with the feature article titled, "Boys in Control" written by Niall Stokes. The next month they got another cover feature in *Record Mirror*, their first outside of Ireland. The band desperately wanted to reach the next level and sign a record deal. They decided to do a two-week club tour of England in December and finance it through a publishing deal, but it fell through at the last minute. Their parents chipped in and they raised just enough cash to get to London. The band played the Moonlight Club, the Hope and Anchor,

Dingwalls, and the Electric Ballroom, supporting the Talking Heads and Orchestral Manoeuvres in the Dark. After all the work, they never got their elusive record deal and had to return to Dublin empty handed. Back in Ireland, they released "Another Day" as a single and went on an Irish tour. One night in March, Paul Morley from *NME* came to see them perform in Cork and was suitably impressed. He later wrote,

> U2 are sharp and subtle and cynical, slyly seductive in an uncompromising way . . . U2 are style plus spontaneity, an uncouth grace, an agile synthesis of abusive and abrasive ways. . . ."[25]

In a surprisingly audacious move, U2 booked themselves into Dublin's National Stadium, which seated about 2,500, for their finale on February 26. They didn't sell it out—roughly 1,000 people showed up—but they performed well and impressed everyone with their moxie. At the end of the gig Nick Stewart from Island Records met them backstage and offered them a deal. Founded by Chris Blackwell, Island had been the home of Bob Marley and had a reputation for allowing more artistic control for the bands it signed. U2 later went to London and, on March 23, 1980, ended up signing their contract in, of all places, the ladies' washroom at the Lyceum Theater. It was for four albums within five years and they were paid 100,000 pounds, with 50,000 each for both recording and touring.[26] The band went to work immediately envisioning their debut album. One producer who came instantly to mind was Martin Hannett, who had worked with Joy Division. At first glance, it seemed both bands couldn't be further apart in style and ethos. But Joy Division was the most influential post-punk band in 1980 and also had a dark, spiritual quality that U2 admired. Arrangements were made for a meeting, and work began on U2's major label debut.

Notes

1. *U2 by U2* (New York: HarperCollins, 2006), 15.
2. Ibid., 18.
3. Visnja Cogan. *U2: An Irish Phenomenon* (Cork: The Collins Press, 2006), 15.
4. Matt McGee. *U2: A Diary* (London: Omnibus Press, 2008), 8.
5. *U2 by U2*, 29.

6. *U2 by U2*, 32.
7. "Easter Rising." August 16, 2001. www.hotpress.com: http://www.hot press.com/archive/1485975.html (accessed April 29, 2009).
8. McGee, 12.
9. "Virgin Prunes: True Life Story." June 9, 2003. www.virginprunes.com: http://www.virginprunes.com/about/name_and_members.html (accessed April 29, 2009).
10. *U2 By U2*, 39.
11. Bill Graham, *U2 The Early Days: Another Time, Another Place* (London: Octopus Publishing Group, 1989), 14.
12. The Clash, "1977."
13. "Reeling In the Years." March 25, 1978. www.hotpress.com: http://www.hotpress.com/archive/549300.html (accessed April 29, 2009).
14. *U2 by U2*, 43.
15. "The Early Years: Three to Under a Blood Red Sky." www.u2faqs.com: http://www.u2faqs.com/history/a.html#1 (accessed April 29, 2009).
16. Michka Assayas. *Bono on Bono* (London: Hodder & Stoughton Ltd., 2005), 94.
17. McGee, 18.
18. "Reeling in the Years." March 25, 1978. www.hotpress.com: http://www .hotpress.com/archive/549300.html?page_no=2&show_comments=1 (accessed April 29, 2009).
19. *U2 by U2*, 65.
20. Graham, 20.
21. Ibid., 25.
22. *U2 by U2*, 72.
23. Graham, 23.
24. "Audio. Bono, August 1979, Irish radio." June 1, 2008. www.youtube .com: http://www.youtube.com/watch?v=K9FlKqCspeg (accessed April 29, 2009).
25. "Paul Morley's 1980 review of U2." December 18, 2005. www.observer .guardian.co.uk: http://observer.guardian.co.uk/omm/story/0,,1667375 ,00.html (accessed April 29, 2009).
26. McGee, 29.

CHAPTER TWO

A New Song: *Boy* & *October* (1980–1982)

Martin Hannett was hot property in 1980. He had been responsible for the haunting sound at the heart of the most respected band of the day, Joy Division. When U2 was considering a producer for their debut, they were invited to the "Love Will Tear Us Apart" sessions to observe Hannett and the band at work. Edge thought everything seemed a bit too precious and mannered for rock and roll, but Joy Division weren't simple posers—they played dark music because that was who they were. When U2 played Hannett their demo for "11 O'Clock Tick Tock," he said he wasn't too impressed with the production, but liked the song. Hannett was invited to Dublin to record the single over the Easter weekend, and they entered Windmill Lane Studios for the first time; Windmill Lane would become U2's home studio for years to come.

The band had some trouble accommodating Hannett's coveted sound and style. Larry and Adam were in for the hardest time, and Edge was a bit surprised at Hannett's seeming indifference to overdubs. In the end, "11 O'Clock Tick Tock" is a great record—a clash of metallic sparks and the template for Edge's signature guitar sound, but not a hit. Either way, the recording was the breakthrough U2 was looking for: it defined their futuristic rock sound and began to separate them from the pack. The idea for the title had come from an expression Gavin Friday used meaning "the end of the day." He had come around to Bono's home one night and left a note on his door with the phrase. It struck a chord with Bono and he filed it away. Later, when Bono was looking over the crowd at a London show of the gothic-psychobilly band the Cramps, he thought they resembled zombies at the end of days and wrote the lyric soon after.[1]

By spring 1980 the band had finally purchased an old van and were touring up and down Ireland and Britain. They stayed in bed-and-breakfasts that veered from nylon sheets to plush cushions. The band had a hard time adjusting to life on the road. Each member had his own approach: Adam enjoyed the late-night parties more than the others, whereas Larry just needed some clean sheets and *Space Invaders* to get through the night. Paul was turning out to be a savvy manager, always on the lookout for anything that might elevate U2's image. One strategy was to try to fill every venue U2 played. He would book the band into places that were a bit smaller than their following would allow, and only agreed to play two nights if U2 could be guaranteed to get a capacity crowd for each show. This helped create a buzz that the band was a big deal, and next time tickets would be in greater demand.

Onstage, U2 was unlike any of their contemporaries. Whereas Joy Division embodied their funereal music in their fashion and demeanor, other bands seemed to be putting on appearances. During the post-punk era it was considered cool to stand around on stage without working up a sweat. U2 reacted against this pose and tried to put on blistering performances whenever they got the chance. Bono would run around the stage and climb on the speakers, whereas bands like Echo and the Bunnymen were content to play it cool and stand still.

After "11 O'Clock Tick Tock" was released in May, U2 began to make plans for their debut album. They had arranged for Hannett to produce, but he was wrapped up with Joy Division. Then when Joy Division singer Ian Curtis committed suicide, plans dissolved. As U2 started looking around for other producers, Steve Lillywhite's name came up. He got his start in 1976 producing a demo for Ultravox and had just finished Peter Gabriel's breakthrough third album, which included the era-defining songs "Games without Frontiers" and "Biko." U2 also admired the work he'd done with XTC and Siouxsie and the Banshees. The band arranged a test session with Lillywhite at Windmill Lane and recorded their second single, "A Day Without Me." It was another great recording with Edge's Memory Man providing an echo riff and Bono's lyric exploring the theme of suicide, an issue Ian Curtis' death had pushed to the fore.

U2 got along very well with Lillywhite and considered him a refreshing change from Hannett. He had more experience and was willing to work within the band's limitations to develop their sound, rather than trying to mask any weaknesses. He was also open to innovative techniques like breaking bottles for sound effects and using a spoon on the spokes of a spinning bicycle wheel for the chime-like percussion on "I Will Follow." Larry recorded his drums under a stairwell because they realized the studio room was smothering the punch of his kit. With Lillywhite's encouragement, he also did overdubs for the first time.

In these early days, Bono wrote spontaneously and often changed a lyric each night depending on his mood. When it came time to commit to a version he would put it off until the last minute. While recording the first album, he found himself struggling to finish the songs. He'd settle on one idea and then discard it the next day. Most of the themes flowed from the concept of boyhood innocence he had been exploring for the past few years in songs like "Stories For Boys" and "Out Of Control." Bono recalls:

> I had a sense that this was subject matter no one else in rock and roll had ever explored—the end of adolescent angst, the elusiveness of being male, the sexuality, spirituality, friendship.[2]

The album was recorded over the spring and summer of 1980 and released in October as *Boy*. The cover was striking for the time and included a photo of Bono's old friend, Guggi's younger brother, Peter Rowan, looking straight out at the camera, the living embodiment of innocence and vulnerability. The band had already been playing over half of the songs for months and their confidence shines through. It's an exhilarating debut, full of force and vision. A voice counts in "1-2-3-4" to kick it off as the grinding two-note riff of "I Will Follow" catches fire, slightly reminiscent of Keith Levene's work on PiL's "Public Image." The percussion twinkles in the background like pixie dust before the drums break through and we're "on the inside" with the band. The rest of the album stands out for Edge's guitar work and Bono's urgent vocals. Another notable track, easily overlooked for its brevity, is "Into the Heart," a shimmering moment of introspection and spiritual lucidity that heralded some of U2's most stirring songs like "40" and "With or Without You."

U2 began another tour of England in September with a professional road crew and the full support of Island Records. The Marquee Club in London was especially memorable as the place where the Who got their start. U2 played there regularly over the fall, and soon they were pulling in a sell-out crowd. After U2's November 27 performance, Gavin Martin from *New Music Express* wrote:

> Only a blind man and the dead could ignore the passion and charisma generated by singer Bono. The very essence which underpins the performance is an electric vibrancy between the stage and the dancefloor. It's something loads of groups try for, but only a few can achieve.[3]

After five weeks of touring, U2 played their first European dates in the Netherlands and Belgium before returning to England. Their final European show was in Paris on December 3, and they then set their sights on the United States. Paul realized that the biggest British groups of the last decade, such as Led Zeppelin and the Who, had a special connection to the United States. Although they may have fallen out of fashion in much of Europe with the rise of punk, in the United States they were still revered. Paul met the legendary promoter Frank Barsalona, head of Premier Talent, which represented the Who and Bruce Springsteen. Paul and Barsalona forged a relationship that would help U2 enormously in the years to come. On December 4, U2 flew into JFK Airport in New York and were driven to the Gramercy Park Hotel in a limo Paul had arranged. They were blown away with the Big Apple and its legendary status as the home to CBGBs, Television, and the Ramones, and Bono would later write about the experience in "Angel Of Harlem." The band spent hours wandering the streets and soaking up the gritty vibe of Manhattan.

U2 played their first U.S. show on December 6, 1980, at the Ritz, two days before John Lennon was assassinated. They were extremely nervous, but according to Barsalona it was a very memorable gig with the band winning over a new section of the crowd with each song they played and getting called back for two encores.[4] This brief tour included only eight dates in the northeast United States, with U2 traveling from city to city crammed inside a rented van. When they rolled into Boston for a show at the Paradise Theater on December 15, they found an eager and supportive audience waiting. Local radio stations had taken an interest in the band and were generating a substantial following. Carter Alan, a local DJ and author of the book *U2:*

Outside Is America, had been one of the very first people on U.S. radio to push U2. Their performance that night was a huge success, with Bono borrowing a few lines from John Lennon's "Give Peace a Chance" and inserting them into "Electric Co." By the end the audience brought them back once again for two encores.[5]

At the end of the tour the band returned to Ireland for Christmas, and in January Edge, Bono, and Larry attended a weekend retreat for Christian musicians in Worcester, England. Bono and Edge gave a 45-minute presentation during which Bono mentioned Isaiah 40:3 and Edge Psalm 40 as verses that they felt were important to U2's calling.[6] The experience of playing in the United States was exhilarating, but it had also opened their eyes to some of the sleaze that comes with rock and roll. After the retreat, U2 continued to tour through January and February. They played in the United Kingdom and Europe, including performing in Sweden, Germany, and Switzerland for the first time. At the end of January, the band met Stuart Adamson from the Skids, and later Big Country, in Edinburgh. At the Lyceum in London, U2 covered Bob Dylan's "All Along the Watchtower" for the first time. In February they received their first mention in *Rolling Stone* magazine with James Henke calling their sound "pop music with brains" and comparing them to the Who and Television. Bono told Henke:

> I don't mean to sound arrogant, but even at this stage, I do feel that we are meant to be one of the great groups. There's a certain spark, a certain chemistry, that was special about the Stones, the Who and the Beatles, and I think it's also special about U2.[7]

The cover for *Boy* had raised some eyebrows, and Island was worried that audiences in the United States might read pedophilia into the photo of the young Peter Rowan. The label changed it to a photocopied image of each band member stretched and distorted out of shape for the North American release in March. U2 returned to the United States for a 7-week, 35-city tour opening in Washington, D.C., on March 3. The *Washington Post* reported:

> U2 brought to their performance a sense of refinement that has been lacking in rock for some time. U2, like the Police and the Clash, are taking new wave to the next, higher musical level.[8]

Paul spent a lot of energy forging close ties with promoters and reps from Warner's and Island Records, and his efforts were paying off.

Barsalona's Premier Talent—one of the most experienced agencies in the business—was booking the tour. U2 received solid support throughout these early years. One reason for this was U2's attitude. They never came off as condescending or arrogant; instead, their natural exuberance was infectious, and unlike many of their peers they sincerely enjoyed meeting people. U2 also enjoyed spending time with fans. On March 22 the band hosted a backstage party in Portland, and Bono left his leather satchel case behind. Panic set in because the contents included his lyric sketches for U2's next album. After a futile search Bono believed it had been stolen; it wasn't until 2004 when two women came forward to return it that he learned he left it behind himself.[9]

U2 was learning about some of the obstacles touring the United States posed. One challenge they faced was differentiating themselves from the pack of British bands that were flooding into the States at the time. U2 was constantly being lumped into a "psychedelic revival" with Liverpool groups like Echo and the Bunnymen and Julian Cope's the Teardrop Explodes. Bono would make a point of saying to audiences that U2 wasn't just another English band passing through—they were Irish and were in the United States for three months.[10] Another challenge was the arid state of U.S. radio. Very few major stations played anything new and were sticking to old stalwarts like REO Speedwagon and Fleetwood Mac. It took college radio to promote the new music, which eventually flourished into the alternative scene of the 1980s. Overall, the band was taken with the width and breadth of the United States. Everything from hamburgers to cars was bigger. So were the wild parties. Adam and Paul spent most of the time socializing while the rest of the band stayed in and sought refuge in prayer meetings. Larry recalls:

> The prayer meetings were a safe haven because they brought us together through some of the ups and downs of being on the road. Except for Adam, he was off having a really good time.[11]

Larry had always been the pretty boy of the band, but when U2 played San Francisco he was surprised to find himself the focus of a gay following. At first he resented it, but soon learned to accept the attention without any worries. U2 took a small break in April to record a new song, "Fire," in the Caribbean with Lillywhite producing. They released it in the UK as a single and debuted it later on the

Top of the Pops in August on a stage resembling a burning cauldron. Ironically, the song began to slide *down* the charts after the show due to their poor performance. After their Caribbean break U2 returned to the United States, picking up the tour in Gainesville, Florida. When Bono was interviewed about his songwriting by Boston radio station WBCN, he replied:

> As a lyric writer, I'm more interested in people than politics and more interested in why people should want to hit each other over the head with a broken bottle rather than where they do it . . . it being Northern Ireland. Everybody is violent, I feel.[12]

At the end of May, U2 appeared on *The Tomorrow Show* with Tom Snyder, their first time on U.S. television, performing "I Will Follow" and "Twilight." Bono walked into the studio audience and brought the crowd to its feet. He joined Edge for a brief interview with Snyder, who predicted, "We will be hearing a great deal about *the* U2 in this country in the months and years to come."[13]

U2 returned to Europe to perform a few gigs in the UK and met Bruce Springsteen and Pete Townsend after a show at London's Hammersmith Palais. The Who had been huge role models for U2, who regarded "My Generation" as the first real *rock* record. There were often comparisons between the two bands in the early days because both shared a similar setup—guitar, bass, drums, and a powerful vocalist. U2 had also been big fans of Springsteen, going back to their early teens. After seeing one of his blistering live performances at Wembley Arena, they were convinced that playing a bigger venue didn't necessarily mean it would dilute the power of the music.

During the summer of 1981, U2 began to work on their second album. *Boy* hadn't cracked the top 50 in the either the UK or the United States, so the pressure was on. After the lyrics went missing in Portland, Bono went crazy trying to squeeze together some new ideas. He had 2 years to prepare for *Boy,* but now he had only 12 weeks for the new album. It didn't help matters that the band was low on cash and didn't have a rehearsal space. They eventually went back to where it all began and, for a small fee, rented a room at their old high school, Mount Temple. Adam, Edge, and Larry began assembling musical bits and pieces, and it was Bono's job to put a melody and lyrics on top of it. He was struggling right up until they went into the studio with Lillywhite to begin recording. They had only three or four songs ready; the rest of the album had to be created on the spot in the studio. Most of the final lyrics on *October* are propelled by images rather than narrative stories. The death of Bono's mother was still on his mind, and it turned up on "Tomorrow" as the "black car outside"—a hearse. At the time Bono also suggested it was about the violence in Northern Ireland, particularly house-to-house assassinations. Bono said:

> The lyrics are like a puzzle because, on *October*, I didn't know what I was saying a lot of the time. Things came out of me on that record that I wasn't even aware were in there. People accuse me of not being specific enough in the lyrics and that is fair criticism, but I think there is more power in imagery because it can do more things—people can react on more levels.[14]

Larry was experimenting with rhythms but was struggling to achieve the avalanche sound of "I Threw A Brick Through a Window." Eventually, Edge recorded a stronger tom-tom part and Larry realized he had to up his game. During the sessions, the band agreed to play an open-air gig in August at Slane Castle outside Dublin with Thin Lizzy, but the new songs bombed. The band was unprepared and ran into technical problems. It was a major setback and it pushed Edge into seriously considering other options. In an attempt to salvage their self-confidence, U2 was a last-minute addition the following week at the Greenbelt Christian Music and Arts Festival in Odell, England. They played a seven-song set with borrowed instruments after Bono believed he had received a message from God telling U2 to play.[15]

As they went back into the studio, Adam became hesitant about the direction of the lyrics. They were taking on an overtly religious tone, almost sermonizing, and dealing directly with Christianity. *October's* opening song, "Gloria," was a rock redux of the ancient Latin hymn "*Gloria in excelsis deo*" and "Tomorrow" explicitly evoked Jesus in the lines "Come back, heal me/ Jesus, come back."[16] Adam was aware of the soul tradition of Aretha Franklin and Marvin Gaye and also of Bob Dylan's recent controversial re-branding as a born-again Christian, but it didn't feel right for a young, new group. He was beginning to feel out of step with the rest of the band.

In every crisis there are the seeds of possibility. U2's concern about the path their lives were taking opened the music up to new directions. During their tours of the United States and Europe they got peppered with questions about being Irish from journalists and fans eager to know their opinions about the violence in Northern Ireland. During the spring of 1981 Bobby Sands, an IRA volunteer, died in Long Kesh prison while on a hunger strike. His death ignited international coverage of the political situation in the North, and U2 was barraged with questions about their stand on the issue. Like most people their age, U2 was repulsed by the carnage and violence, but they hadn't applied any serious analysis yet. The queries had an effect, and they made the band conscious of who they were and where they fit in as young, Irish men. U2 has always been careful about joining any cause or movement. They have never really been punk, new wave, or post-punk; instead, they've mixed and matched genres based on whatever came naturally. Being an Irish band gave them a unique perspective unlike any of their UK contemporaries—rock music wasn't seen as the enemy in Ireland as it was in England. U2 has always asked to be judged on the merits of their music and to not be compared with others or boxed into any category. The same caution applied to politics. Just because U2 was Irish didn't mean they automatically sympathized with the IRA. They understood the root cause had much to do with the British government, but were torn about what they could do. When fans would throw the Irish tricolour flag on stage, Bono was known to strip off the orange and green and wave the remaining white strip, drained, he said, of any nationalism.

The sound of Vinnie Kilduff's uilleann pipes at the beginning of "Tomorrow" was one response to the band's introspective searching. The pipes are a quintessential Irish sound dating back centuries, and in 1982 they were identified more with the folk tradition than anything to do with rock. It was an extraordinary addition that predated Ireland's folk resurgence later in the 1980s, when traditional performers like the Dubliners and Chieftains joined forces with the Pogues and Sinead O'Connor to revitalize Irish music.

Bono had the idea for the album title, *October,* before the song was written. He felt it represented the stripping away of sentiment and comfort and embodied the coldness of the 1980s.[17] Edge hadn't played much piano since he was young, so when he wrote "October" it came as a bit of a surprise. He had been inspired by U2's tour of Europe, during which he felt more European than he ever had before. "October" was his attempt to capture the stark utility of what he had seen in parts of Amsterdam and Berlin. He was also deeply involved with the Christian group Shalom and feeling conflicted over his future with the band.

October opens with the triumphant "Gloria," a firm affirmation of Christian belief with Bono providing a strident coda influenced by an album of Gregorian chants he had borrowed from Paul. The next two tracks, "I Fall Down" and "I Threw a Brick Through a Window," reflect more self-doubt and violence than faith. Bono recalls:

> There was a row in the house. I remember throwing a carving knife at my brother and it sticking in the door. I missed—but that's what "I Threw a Brick through a Window" was about.[18]

The rest of the album continues this mix of religious fervor and spiritual yearning until the icy piano of "October" offers a cool respite. "With A Shout" is one of the band's most brazenly Christian songs, with a misplaced brass section, while "Scarlet" revisits the spiritual shimmerings heard before on *Boy*'s "Into The Heart." For the cover, the band had their photo taken at the Dublin docklands, but Island tried to dissuade them from using it. The band refused. It's a ponderous shot of the four with a rundown factory across the River Liffey in the background. It was an austere antidote to the glossy images of the New Romantics coming from England at the time, and signaled the earnest commitment that would become U2's hallmark throughout the 1980s. *October* was released in the same month as its title, to mixed reviews. Neil McCormick in *Hot Press* wrote:

> It is a Christian LP that avoids all the pedantic puritanism associated with most Christian rock, avoids the old world emotional fascism of organised religion and the crusading preaching of someone like born-again Bob Dylan.[19]

October failed to sell as well as *Boy*, peaking at number 11 in the UK and 104 in the United States. U2 could have been dropped from Island, but they were kept on and steeled themselves for another tour. Before heading out, the band filmed a video for "Gloria" directed by Meiert Avis, who had filmed an in-studio video for "I Will Follow" the previous year. U2 performed for a small crowd on the River Liffey— the same location as the album cover—floating on a barge under slate-gray skies. It's an interesting slice of the nascent video format. Bono sports a streaked mullet predating Bon Jovi's by about six years, as Edge plays a bit of slide guitar, Adam pops a few notes, and Larry's rhythm holds the song steady. It turned out to be quite successful and MTV, launched in August of 1981, included it on heavy rotation.

Throughout October U2 toured the UK and Europe, finishing in Berlin at the beginning of November. Back in Dublin, Bono, Edge, and Larry were still attending Shalom meetings. The gatherings were becoming intense, placing more emphasis on total commitment and questioning their involvement in rock and roll. Larry resented the pressure and quit Shalom. Edge, however, quit U2, and only told Bono, who decided to join him. Edge recalls:

> It was a very, very clear fork on the road really. We were listening to all this negativity from people who were supposed to be our friends, telling us we can't continue in this band, it's not right. So I took a bit of time to get it straight in my own head who was to be trusted.[20]

The band had a meeting and it turned into a bit of a showdown. Paul was shocked when he heard their plans, and challenged the belief that they would be more effective doing God's work in their normal lives. He emphasized the power of the music to reach thousands, if not millions, of people, and also spoke about their commitments to Island and everyone involved in the upcoming tour. In the end, Paul convinced Edge and Bono to stay with U2. It was wrong to think rock and roll and spirituality couldn't mix, and they recognized that music was their way of worshipping God. Now they were determined to prove it.

After the showdown, U2 arrived in New York for a five-week tour in November. A few nights later in New Haven, Connecticut, Bono and Larry almost got into a fight on stage when Larry was having trouble with his kit and kept missing his cue. Bono blew his cool, pushed the drums into the audience, and ran after Larry. Edge stepped in and ended up punching Bono, bringing to an end the sudden outburst. The pressures of the road were obviously taking their toll. In some cities they found they hardly drew a crowd, whereas in others, such as Los Angeles, U2 could sell out depending on radio support. The constant gigging had an effect and was sharpening their skills. When they returned to London in late December they played the Lyceum with the Alarm, delivering a blistering show *Record Mirror* called "the gig of 1981."[21]

During their Christmas break they recorded another song, "A Celebration," with "Trash, Trampoline and the Party Girl" on the B-side.

They also cut a video and released it in early 1982 to fill the gap left by *October*'s lack of singles. Larry recalls:

> We went to this prison in Dublin, where the 1916 uprising took place, called Kilmainham Jail, and filmed it with the idea of breaking out. It was very much a look at ourselves. Like when we were in school and everyone was telling us 'you're crap' and we couldn't get a record deal—it was the triumph of breaking through.[22]

Declan Lynch, writing in *Hot Press*, spelled out his distaste for the song:

> Now I'm aware that we all live in little boxes and that we drink too much and back horses too much, but U-2's version of spiritual abandon harks back to the catechism—a few catch-phrases never freed a spider from his web . . . U-2 might try to develop a few inhibitions.[23]

The B-side, "Party Girl," as it was to become known, has stood the test of time better than "A Celebration," eventually turning up on various set lists over the years.

U2 returned to the United States in February, and while playing onboard a riverboat in New Orleans they met a visionary who would transform their raw image into the cool, grainy tones that became their iconic signature during the eighties. Anton Corbijn had been working as a photographer for *NME* and had worked with Joy Division and Public Image. Bono describes Corbijn's photos as an attempt to portray the band as they might be, not as they were. It was like he was taking pictures of the music rather than the musicians.[24]

In March U2 was invited to play 14 shows opening for the J. Geils Band. Fronted by Peter Wolf, the J. Geils Band had a number one record called "Centerfold" and had just finished opening for the Rolling Stones on their 1981 U.S. tour. They had an older, bluesier crowd, but it gave U2 the chance to play arenas for the first time and reach audiences they never would have otherwise.

On March 17 Paul had arranged for the band to appear in New York's St. Patrick's Day parade, but the plans fell apart when he learned that Irish hunger striker Bobby Sands was to be named honorary grand marshall. U2 was firm that they didn't want to be associated with anything that could be construed as being sympathetic to the IRA.[25] By now the band had run out of money and had to rely on Paul's credit card to fly home and pay the crew. It was frustrating to have released two albums and done as many tours, and still not have anything to show for it.

Back in Ireland they played only 10 shows between March and August before hunkering down to begin work on their third album. They rented a place in Howth in northern Dublin and moved in together for a time. Ali and Bono got married on August 21; Adam served as best man. Bono chose Adam because he felt the need to connect with him on a deeper level. The newlyweds then moved into the house together with the band. For their honeymoon, Bono and Ali went to Jamaica and stayed in Chris Blackwell's "Goldeneye" home, where Bono continued working on the lyrics for the upcoming album.

Notes

1. Niall Stokes. *U2: Into the Heart* (London: Carlton Books, 2005), 189.
2. *U2 by U2* (New York: HarperCollins, 2006), 100.
3. "U2: Marquee Club." Gavin Murphy. November 30, 1980. www.u2tours .com: http://www.u2tours.com/displaymedia.src?ID=19801127&XID =105&Return (accessed April 29, 2009).
4. Carter Alan, *Outside Is America: U2 in the US* (Boston: Faber and Faber, 1992), 25.
5. Ibid., 20.
6. McGee, 39.
7. "U2: Here Comes the 'Next Big Thing.'" February 19, 1981. www.rolling stone.com: http://www.rollingstone.com/news/story/7088993/u2_here _comes_the_next_big_thing (accessed April 29, 2009).
8. *Washington Post* in Alan, 30.
9. McGee, 42.
10. "U2 Versus the US." April 25, 1981. www.hotpress.com: http://www .hotpress.com/archive/549146.html (accessed April 29, 2009).
11. *U2 by U2*, 110.
12. Alan, 33.
13. "U2—The Tomorrow Show 1981." July 25, 2006. http://www.youtube .com/watch?v=wwHq5iipazw (accessed April 29, 2009).
14. Alan, 36.
15. McGee, 46.
16. *U2 by U2*, 116.
17. Ibid., 120.

18. Stokes, 26.
19. "Autumn Fire." October 10, 1981. www.hotpress.com: http://www.hot press.com/archive/549171.html (accessed April 29, 2009).
20. *U2 by U2*, 118.
21. McGee, 53.
22. "Larry Interview—'83." April 1, 1983. www.u2_interviews.tripod.com: http://u2_interviews.tripod.com/id18.html (accessed April 29, 2009).
23. "Reeling In The Years." October 16, 1981. www.hotpress.com: http:// www.hotpress.com/archive/549300.html?page_no=4&show_comments =1 (accessed April 29, 2009).
24. *U2 by U2*, 127.
25. McGee, 57–58.

CHAPTER THREE

Out of Control: *War* & Commercial Success (1982–1983)

Touring for the last two years had profoundly altered U2's outlook and perceptions of the world. They had always responded to the exuberance of punk and to the spirit of possibilities that the bands of the 1960s embodied; now they had grown up and were prepared to tackle anything the world threw at them. By the summer of 1982, U2 had been playing together for eight years, collectively enduring both ups and downs; they had reached a stage of maturity. On their next album they were determined to move into more complex areas to test the mettle of their faith.

During his honeymoon in Jamaica, Bono used the time away to work on some new ideas for lyrics. U2 had become much tighter from being on the road through 1981 and 1982 and were at their strongest yet. Adam felt he and Larry had come into their own and were ready to take some of the pressure off Edge. During the two weeks Bono was away, Edge came up with sketches for four new songs—"New Year's Day," "Seconds," "Drowning Man," and "Sunday Bloody Sunday."

When Bono returned, the band went into Windmill Lane Studios to flesh out their ideas for a new song they felt was special, "Sunday Bloody Sunday." Steve Lillywhite was reluctant at first to work with the band again, and felt they would benefit more if they tried out a different producer. U2 had tried a few others, namely Sandy Pearlman who produced Blue Öyster Cult and the Clash's *Give 'Em Enough Rope*, but nothing came from the sessions. They also tried

Bill Whelan, who had worked on *October,* and Jimmy Destri, the keyboard player from *Blondie,* but in the end they called up Lillywhite again and he finally agreed.

Their focus was to bring things back to basics and to get away from the grand gestures and triumphal posturing that had characterized much of *October.* Edge laid off the echo and Larry worked hard at tightening the rhythm. Lillywhite felt Larry sped up while playing and urged him to work with a click track to help steady his beat. After initially refusing, Larry bumped into the veteran session drummer Andy Newmark, who had played with David Gilmour and Roxy Music and swore by the click. Larry changed his mind soon after.

By 1982, radio had become stale and clogged up with United Kingdom bands like Spandau Ballet and Duran Duran and American rockers Van Halen and John Cougar. Post-punk, the movement that U2 was initially lumped in with, shunned the type of fame U2 sought. Bands like Joy Division, Gang of Four, and the Fall were hugely influential, but they spurned commercial success. Part of this had to do with the politics of the times. America had fallen out of fashion with radio's attachment to corporate rock, its resistance to "New Wave," and the inauguration of Ronald Reagan in January 1981. Post-punk bands were looking east to Berlin for inspiration where David Bowie had recorded his "Berlin Trilogy," including *Low* and *Heroes,* with Brian Eno a few years earlier.

However, U2 understood that the United States held the key to becoming the world's greatest band, and they wouldn't let any dogma hold them back. With their new album U2 wanted to clear the decks and declare war on all that was trivial and backward-looking. They were also becoming acutely aware of the world around them and realizing how little they truly knew about it. For a band like U2, it was impossible not to care about events, whether in Ireland or Eastern Europe, and they were becoming increasingly politicized. They were carrying on the tradition of other socially aware bands like the Gang of Four and, especially, the Clash, who had released their three-album tour de force, *Sandinista,* just over a year earlier. Part of this process involved staking out a position on the IRA and British forces in Northern Ireland, commonly referred to as "the troubles." According to Bono:

> It was only when I realized that the troubles hadn't affected me that they began to affect me. The bombs may not go off in Dublin but they're made here.[1]

Edge had come up with the idea of Northern Ireland for the song, "Sunday Bloody Sunday." It originally included the lines "don't talk to me about the rights of the IRA,"[2] but the band felt it was too one-sided. Bono turned to Irish history and the original lyrics were rewritten to reflect a less sectarian bent. U2 was in a unique position to address the complexities of conflict. Bono came from a mixed Protestant and Catholic home. Bob, his father, had agreed to raise Bono and his elder brother Norman as Catholics in accordance with his wife, Iris's, wishes. Edge and Adam had been born in England and even retained a bit of their English accents, whereas Larry came from an Irish Catholic family. Mount Temple was a nondenominational high school, and the students were naturally inclined to look beyond religion as an identifying characteristic. The band was instinctively aware of the complexities of the violence occurring in the name of republicanism or unionism, but refused to be silent. Instead, U2 took a position that both sides had it wrong and passionately supported an end to the fighting. It was a brave stand to take in the midst of what many saw as a battle with no middle ground. Even Ireland's foremost poet, W. B. Yeats, had encouraged bloodletting as a legitimate way to foster the nation in "The Rose Tree": "There's nothing but our own red blood/ Can make a right Rose Tree." The rose was a symbol for Ireland and Yeats wrote this following the Easter Rising of 1916. U2 was up against a formidable tradition. As usual, they chose the more difficult path, but one that was morally consistent with their principles.

The title "Sunday Bloody Sunday" refers to two events—the 1922 massacre of more than 30 people in Dublin's Croke Park, and the 1972 massacre of 14 in Derry, Northern Ireland. The song shares the same title as John Lennon and Yoko Ono's 1972 recording from their album *Some Time In New York City,* but differs in content. Rather than take sides, U2 expresses a more humanitarian viewpoint, refusing to "heed the battle call," but its tone is one of grit and anger. Before playing it live, Bono would begin by declaring it wasn't a rebel song. The final version of "Sunday Bloody Sunday" is an example of U2's aggressive pacifism, a protest against the continuing cycle of violence that was claiming lives on both sides of the conflict.

During the recording of *War,* Bono kept nagging Edge to ease off the atmospherics and rock out like Mick Jones from the Clash.[3] Edge took up the challenge and sharpened his attack. On "Sunday Bloody Sunday" his playing is as raw and serrated as razor wire. Larry's new-found discipline from playing with a click-track, together with his earlier training in the Artane and Post Office bands, helped him come up with the song's hook—the military salvo that cracks open the song and U2's third album. "Sunday Bloody Sunday," U2's first overtly political song, was also a battle cry from the gut declaring that they were a different band from the one that had made *Boy* and *October*.

During the sessions, Edge met a young man at a bus stop carrying a violin case. Steve Wickham, who would soon go on to join the seminal-root bands In Tua Nua and the Waterboys, was a U2 fan and suggested the band might use a violin on their new album. Edge agreed, and three days later Wickham was in the studio working on "Sunday Bloody Sunday" and "Drowning Man."[4] *War* represented a bold step forward musically for the band. It incorporated elements of folk, funk, and female vocalists—Kid Creole's Coconuts. "Seconds" even includes a sample from Nick Broomfield's 1982 documentary *Soldier Girls*: "I want to be an airborne ranger/ I want to live a life of danger." It was a prescient inclusion and foreshadowed the sampling craze that eventually overtook hip-hop and pop later in the decade. U2 recognized how the studio could be used as an instrument, realizing that recording was an art form in and of itself, completely different from performing live.

The album's first single, "New Year's Day," featured one of Adam's most memorable bass lines—the slithering riff throbbing beneath Bono's provocative lyric, "And we're told this is the golden age/ Gold is reason for the wars we wage." The couplet encapsulated U2's feelings about the state of the world in 1982. Despite the luxuries of the West, the world seemed consumed by conflict: Britain was battling Argentina in a pointless war over the Falkland Islands, Israel had invaded Lebanon, and the Cold War between the United States and the USSR continued to raise the specter of nuclear annihilation. Tensions were also high in Poland, where the Solidarity movement was challenging the Soviet-backed government. As with many early songs, Bono felt the lyric was sloppy and unfocused. Regardless, "New Year's Day" managed to embrace both the personal and the political, referring to the Polish Solidarity movement and to his new life with Ali.

Edge's acoustic guitar, along with Wickham's violin and a string section, distinguished "Drowning Man." Bono borrowed snippets of the lyrics from Isaiah 40:31: "They shall mount up with wings as eagles; they shall run and not be weary." It was a track Edge felt particularly proud of:

Whereas I know some of the songs on the *War* album could be re-recorded and improved on, with "Drowning Man" it's perfection for that song. It's one of the most successful pieces of recording we've ever done.[5]

War took three months to record, but on the last day U2 found they were one song short. They worked all through the night and began recording at six in the morning, two hours before the next band was scheduled to take over the studio. Lillywhite pulled out a promising track, but it had too many time changes and the band was at a loss over what to do with it. Bono opened a Bible that was lying around the studio and chose the Psalm 40 for the lyric. Adam had stepped out of the studio, so Edge filled in on bass adding a supple, melodic riff. Bono recorded the vocal track and the final mix was done within an hour. "40" would go on to become the band's signature song throughout the 1980s. It was the final song in their set, and would cause audiences from Sheffield to Los Angeles to sing the refrain, which echoes "Sunday Bloody Sunday," again and again: "How long to sing this song, how long?"

There is an air of desperation, hope, and militant urgency bleeding throughout the album's 10 tracks. The cover is a rebuke of their debut's image of innocence with a now-battered and traumatized Peter Rowan staring out accusingly, a casualty of some unseen conflict. Anton Corbijn's black and white photos of the band in the snow only enhance the album's chilling siege mentality. With *War*, U2 had made their peace with religion and no longer felt the need to sermonize as overtly as before. Larry said,

> It's a personal thing. If you talk to a person about it, you should be telling *him*, not the public at large. It shouldn't be an angle.[6]

Edge went further; "All religion seems to do is divide. I'm really interested in and influenced by the spiritual side of Christianity, rather than the legislative side, the rules and regulations."[7] *War* represents the first time the band had truly come together, with each member delivering his best studio performance to date. They all realized they had achieved something special, but just how special was yet to be seen.

In November, and in keeping with the political theme of *War*, U2 gave their first endorsement for a politician when the leader of the Fine Gael Party, Garret Fitzgerald, dropped by Windmill Lane for a photo op. It made quite a stir in Ireland at the time, and soon after Fitzgerald won the race for the Taoiseach, Ireland's head of government.

Before the album was released, U2 did a pre-*War* tour during December to test out the new songs. While in Sweden they found the conditions right to make a video and grabbed director Meiert Avis again. They hopped into a couple of small planes and flew 400 miles north of Stockholm to Salen to shoot the video for "New Year's Day." It was 10 degrees below zero, extremely cold, but they were determined to maintain an elemental feel for the video, and the snow was a perfect visual for the clear, icy tones of the song. The final video was like a sweeping scene from Dr. Zhivago, but the iconic scene of the band riding horses over the tundra was done by female extras—the band didn't know how to ride. Avis's video captured the imagination of fans, and by January 1983 "New Year's Day" was a top-10 hit in the UK. It many ways it embodied the antithesis of the times—the day-glow splashes of color and the life of comfort the New Romantic bands were indulging in seemed like mindless distractions by comparison.

After U2 returned to Ireland and were playing in Belfast, they were concerned about how "Sunday Bloody Sunday" would be received. In recent years, this had been the epicenter for the conflict that had torn the Irish apart for centuries, and here were a bunch of youths barely out of their teens daring to suggest they had the answers. Bono introduced it to the audience:

> Listen, this is called "Sunday Bloody Sunday." It's not a rebel song. It's a song of hope and a song of disgust. We're gonna play it for you here in Belfast. If you don't like it, you let us know.[8]

The crowd loved it and was ecstatic in their approval. U2 went on to play "New Year's Day" on *Top Of the Pops* in late January, showcasing their new confidence and sound. In Dundee, Scotland, on February 26, U2 played "40" for the first time live, beginning a tradition of closing the show with the crowd joining in on the refrain. When the album was released in the UK at the end of February, it went straight to number one. By now they had three charting singles—"Fire," "Gloria," and "A Celebration"—but they hadn't yet made the U.S. charts, where they were still considered an underground band. As they embarked on their next world tour, the image of the white flag became a dominant motif. It was a symbol of nonviolence and also a surrendering to forces larger than themselves. In a later interview the band explained how the use of the flag was related to *War*'s main theme of surrender. Adam explained his feelings:

I think surrender in itself sounds like a very weak thing to do, but basically . . . you have to find out your feelings on an issue, and to have an opinion on an issue is usually passion from somewhere within you that you're not going to give up and you have to surrender those passions to be able to see somebody else's point of view, to be able to give in and accept another way of life and that's what that theme is.[9]

In the middle of March, *War* bumped Michael Jackson's *Thriller* from the number one spot on the UK charts, and later that month at the Hammersmith Palais in London, Mike Peters from the Alarm and Big Country's Stuart Adamson joined Bono onstage for Bob Dylan's "Knockin' On Heaven's Door." As the tour picked up momentum U2's shows were becoming more intense, and the new material was pushing Bono to put himself on the line like never before. The positive reaction from European audiences caused him to make some exhilarating, even dangerous gestures on stage. He began climbing the scaffolding surrounding the stage and leaping into the audience. It was his way of engaging those at the back of the crowd who might not be paying much attention to what was happening onstage. Filled with an almost messianic passion, part of this exuberance was related to Bono's convictions about *War*'s relevance to rock history:

I believe that more than any other record, *War* is right for its time. It is a slap in the face against the snap, crackle and pop. John Lennon was right about that kind of music; he called it 'wallpaper music.' Very pretty. Very well designed. Music to eat your breakfast to.[10]

At the beginning of April, U2 was in Paris to shoot the video for "Two Hearts Beat as One" in front of the Sacré-Cœur Basilica. Anton Corbijn was also there to do a shoot, and one photo was eventually used the following year for the cover for the single "Pride (In the Name of Love)." On April 21, U2 flew to New York to embark on a three-month U.S. tour playing in remote, faraway locales, opening for wet T-shirt contests and other bizarre headliners. They grew to appreciate the country's diversity and managed to cocoon themselves away from the drugs and sex that were afflicting other bands. "New Year's Day" was receiving ample radio play, as was the video on MTV. By late April the song had reached number two on the *Radio and Records* AOR chart. Bono told *Rolling Stone:*

Revolution starts at home, in your heart, in your refusal to compromise your beliefs and your values. I'm not interested in politics like people fighting back with sticks and stones, but in the politics of love. I think there is nothing more radical than two peoples loving each other, because it's so infrequent.[11]

Within two weeks of putting on scalding performances in the northeastern United States, Bono damaged his voice. He went to see the doctor of Welsh singer Tom Jones, who ordered him not to do any talking in between shows. It was like telling a camel not to chew with its mouth open, but he relented for the sake of his voice.

U2's musical tastes were becoming more eclectic at this time as the touring introduced them to new influences. Edge had recently appeared on former PiL bassist Jah Wobble's mini LP, *Snake Charmer*, and Larry was listening to early Bob Dylan. When asked about the issue of Northern Ireland, he explained that Americans didn't understand it:

They call it a 'religious war,' but it has nothing to do with religion. It's like the Dylan song "With God On Our Side." During the hunger strikes, the IRA would say, 'God is with me. I went to Mass every Sunday.' And the Unionists said virtually the same thing. And then they'd go out and murder each other. It's very hypocritical.[12]

After his voice healed, Bono continued to up the ante with each show and was taking more and more chances. He would wow audiences by climbing far above the stage to find the highest spot to wave U2's iconic white flag. He was also introducing new dynamics into the songs, singing Chubby Checker's "Let's Twist Again" as well as couplets from "Send in the Clowns" during "The Electric Co." He would lead the audience in chants of "No more! No more!" during "Sunday Bloody Sunday" and pull young women from the audience to dance on stage. All these gestures reflected Bono's commitment to his audience as well as his willingness to go the distance to give them his best performance. U2 has always demonstrated their appreciation for their fans, going out of their way to include the audience in their performances. It's never been unusual to find Bono chatting with a few young fans while journalists wait for a formal interview. One of the ways U2 has always stood out from other bands and cultivated such a loyal following over the years is through their dedication to their fans.

At the end of May U2 played to their biggest crowd yet. They shared the stage with fellow "rockers" David Bowie, the Pretenders, and Stevie Nicks at the four-day US Festival's "Rock Day." The Clash had played two days earlier on "New Wave Day" with INXS, led by future friend, lead singer Michael Hutchence. During their 50-minute midday set, Bono made the best use of the huge stage and the 300,000-plus crowd. He climbed over 100 feet above the stage during "The Electric Co." and began improvising, "I love the crowd, send in the crowd" to the tune of "Send in the Clowns." After waving a white flag, he tossed it into the audience and climbed down. Another of Bono's grand gestures, it became one of the most talked about events of the entire festival.

Realizing their live shows were catching fire, U2 decided they wanted to capture their performance on film. They chose the middle of the country, near Denver at Red Rocks outdoor amphitheater high in the Colorado mountains. They had seen it before on their 1981 tour, but weren't popular enough to play it. The location held 7,000, and they were now confident that they could fill it to capacity. U2 had been gathering a huge cult following, and word was spreading about their incendiary live performances. Paul brought a production team over from the UK to film it, and poured all the band's money into making the show.

The show was set for June 5, but it rained on the day of the performance. Everything was in place, and Paul and the band refused to cancel despite enormous pressure from promoters and crew. Ellen Darst, formerly of U2's U.S. management office, recalled:

> It was a big gamble. That's one thing about Paul—he's a terrific gambler. It was like $250,000. It seemed like a fortune because it was everything they had. This would have been nerve-racking enough, but for the fact it poured! I'll tell you something about this band—the more screwed up things are, the worse the odds are, the better they will be.[13]

Two hours before they were set to begin, the rain let up and was replaced by a misty haze. It created an incredible visual effect and played to U2's strengths. Torches had been placed above the stage along the rocky crags of the amphitheater, creating a crimson glow when reflected against the low-hanging clouds. It was a stunning visual leading to the eventual live album title *Under a Blood Red Sky.*

The crowd turnout was smaller than expected—about 5,000—but those who attended were diehard fans. U2 promised those who couldn't make the trip a free indoor show the next night in Denver. The film became *U2 at Red Rocks* and it set a new benchmark for the band, putting them in a separate league from their peers. It became a regular fixture on MTV, significantly raising U2's profile over other bands that were struggling just to get a song on the radio.

A few weeks later, when U2 played the Los Angeles Sports Arena, Bono climbed up into the balcony and then jumped 20 feet down to the crowd. He was lucky to be caught without anyone getting hurt, but his antics were starting to worry the band, who thought he might not only injure himself, but also others. They were also concerned that his behavior was distracting people from the music. Paul spoke to him, as well as the record company, and Bono agreed to stop, but he couldn't help himself. His reaction to the music was visceral, and he found it impossible to stay contained behind a microphone.

During the tour the band was asked by the Chicago Peace Museum to contribute to an upcoming exhibition, called "Give Peace a Chance," showcasing artists like John Lennon and Stevie Wonder who promoted peace through their music. The museum already contained exhibitions on Martin Luther King Jr. and the civil rights movement, as well as first-hand accounts from the Japanese survivors of the Hiroshima and Nagasaki nuclear attacks called "The Unforgettable Fire." The band was thrilled to have been invited, and agreed to donate the original handwritten manuscript for "New Year's Day," one of its white flags from the tour, and the stage backdrop of the *War* cover. "Give Peace a Chance" opened on September 11, 1983, and also featured the art of Woody Guthrie, Bob Dylan, and many others. Much later, in 1987, Bono donated "Dreams in a Box," a poem he wrote in a Phoenix hotel, to the museum.[14]

The U.S. tour wrapped up June 29 in New York; U2 had made their first profit. They returned to Dublin, but left soon after to play the Werchter Festival in Belgium with Simple Minds and the Eurythmics. Edge and his long-time girlfriend, Aislinn, got married on July 12. They went to Sri Lanka for their honeymoon just as the civil war broke out between the Tamil separatists and the Sinhalese-dominated government. In August, Bono was invited by Irish Prime Minister Garrett Fitzgerald to join a committee on unemployment, but he quickly became disillusioned, saying, "They had another language, committee-speak, and it wasn't mine."[15]

The band reconvened on August 14 to headline the "Day at the Races" concert at Dublin's Phoenix Park. It was a true homecoming show, with Bono bringing his father, Bob, out on stage. They then traveled to Germany to play the Lorelei Rockpalast Festival and had their performance recorded. They were impressed with the results and included six tracks for the forthcoming Jimmy Iovine–produced, eight-song, live mini-LP, *Under a Blood Red Sky*. It was released on November 21, and U2 lobbied for it to be sold for the reduced price of $4.98 rather than the usual eight or nine dollar price. On the original release, "The Electric Co." contained Bono singing a portion of Stephen Sondheim's "Send in the Clowns," but the band hadn't obtained permission. They were in danger of being sued for breach of copyright, and settled the dispute by paying $50,000 and agreeing to remove the 27-second snippet from subsequent pressings.

The band then took September and October off before flying to Japan via Hawaii for their first-ever Japanese show in Osaka on November 22. The fans went wild and the band felt as though they were being idolized like a boy band. When U2 pulled into a train station Bono mistook the screams of fans for the train's screeching wheels, and while walking around the streets of Japan Larry and his girlfriend, Ann, would frequently get stopped for a photograph because they were both blonde.[16]

The luxury and frivolity that accompanied tours was beginning to grate on the band. Bono had been reading up on Malcolm X and Martin Luther King Jr., trying to go deeper behind the glitz and glamour of the United States to fathom what made the country tick. During a stopover show in Hawaii on November 16, the band started to piece together a new song during the sound check, one that would become their next album's biggest hit—"Pride (In the Name of Love)."[17]

NOTES

1. Stokes, 37.
2. *Rolling Stone. U2: The Ultimate Compendium of Interviews, Articles, Facts and Opinions* (New York: Hyperion, 1994), 13.
3. "Steve Lillywhite on Producing U2's 'War.'" July 21, 2008. www.npr.org: http://www.npr.org/templates/story/story.php?storyId=91380167 (accessed April 29, 2009).

4. *U2 by U2*, 135.
5. Alan, 53.
6. *Rolling Stone*, 14.
7. Ibid., 14.
8. Ibid., 13.
9. "U2 Rockpalast Backstage 1983 Interview." April 5, 2009. www
   .youtubecom: http://www.youtube.com/watch?v=uhEresbOsJ8 (accessed
   April 29, 2009).
10. *Rolling Stone*, 15.
11. Ibid., 10.
12. Alan, 50.
13. Carter, 75-76.
14. Carter, 83-84.
15. McGee, 71.
16. *U2 by U2*, 145.
17. McGee, 72.

CHAPTER FOUR

Wide Awake: *The Unforgettable Fire* & Rebirth (1984–1986)

When the band returned from Japan, they played their final show of the tour at London's Victoria Apollo on December 18. After taking a few months off, they began working on their fourth studio album, *The Unforgettable Fire*. The success of the *War* tour had finally made them some money and they were ready to enjoy it. Edge and his wife, Aislinn, had a daughter and bought a home. Bono and Ali moved into a Martello Tower in Bray, just outside Dublin, Adam purchased a house, and Larry bought a motorcycle.

U2 decided not to work with Steve Lillywhite for the next album. Doing so might have helped them achieve even greater fame, but something didn't feel right. They'd been with Lillywhite since before their first album, and he had been encouraging them to work with other producers. They didn't want to get trapped into repeating a formula—the time was right to strike out in a new direction. They considered Jimmy Iovine, who had produced *Under a Blood Red Sky*, and began initiating discussions.[1] They also thought about the German producer Conny Plank, who had worked with Kraftwerk and Brian Eno. They were also fans of Roxy Music and David Bowie and zeroed in on the common denominator: Brian Eno. He had played synthesizer keyboard in the early seventies with Roxy and collaborated on Bowie's "Berlin Trilogy": *Low*, *Heroes*, and *Lodger*. Eno had created a substantial body of solo work himself and, more recently, had been working with the Talking Heads and then David Byrne on the 1981 groundbreaking album, *My Life in the Bush of Ghosts.* Eno was very highly regarded among the musical cognoscenti and infused anything he worked on with integrity and invention.

When Paul contacted Eno, he wasn't interested. But Bono tried and worked his charm, and Eno finally agreed to a meeting. They met in Dublin and Eno had brought along his engineer, Daniel Lanois, with the intention of handing over the project to him. Eno didn't know much about U2, but assumed they were an uninteresting rock band, not inclined to any of the innovations and sonic textures he had been exploring. Bono recalls:

> We played him *Under a Blood Red Sky*, the Red Rocks show, and his eyes glazed over. I now realize how awful the sight of a rock band in full flight was to Brian. But he caught something in the spirit of the band that perked his interest.[2]

The conversation shifted to process—the steps involved in recording—and to the interaction of the musicians involved. Eno was interested in capturing the living acoustics of the recording environment and was eager to move out of studios in a quest to find more creative spaces. U2 shared this interest, and explained they had been rehearsing in Bono's Martello Tower. According to Edge:

> Instead of recording in an acoustically dead environment and trying to revitalize the sound using technology, we would record in a situation which offered very alive acoustics. We would try to control that natural ambience using the technology that we would bring in.[3]

By the end of the meeting, Eno was sold—both he and Lanois agreed to jointly work on the new album. When Chris Blackwell, head of Island Records, found out about the decision, he did something he had never done before: he tried to talk U2 out of it. Eno had a reputation for taking unusual detours, thought Blackwell, and he feared that U2's commercial success would be sabotaged. U2 stood firm, assuring him Eno was the producer they wanted, and Blackwell backed down.

U2 started to look into rehearsal spaces for something more comfortable than Windmill Lane Studios. Around this time, Paul met the owner of Slane Castle, Lord Henry Mountcharles, an Irish aristocrat turned rock promoter. U2 had played with Thin Lizzy at the castle while recording *October* and they seized on the chance to record there when Mountcharles offered it. On May 7 they moved in, choosing the main ballroom with its high ceiling for their rehearsal space. They soon discovered all the rooms had their own unique ambience, and Edge even mic'd his amp outside on a balcony.

Slane Castle was an hour north of Dublin, and it gave the band some room without taking them away from their friends and families. Barry Devlin, the former bass player of Horslips and the producer of U2's second demo back in 1978, was invited to visit Slane and shoot a 30-minute video, *The Making of the Unforgettable Fire*. It contains some behind-the-scenes moments showing the band recording, stretching out on the roof playing guitar, and joking around with some neighborhood kids while watching an eclipse. At one point, Eno is asked about his first impressions of U2:

> My first impression of U2 and my lasting impression of U2 was that they were a band in a way that very few people are bands now. The music was a result of those four people, not those four instruments.[4]

U2 was beginning to develop a vision for their new sound, one that involved bigger, more complex themes than before. Eno would help them achieve this, and together they would prove how versatile a rock band could be. As Bono said:

> Every great rock band in the British invasion went to art school. We never did, we went to Brian. He catalyzed our songwriting, allowed us to get away from the primary colours of rock into another world where we could really describe ourselves in what was going on around us. It was monumental.[5]

Eno and Lanois put the emphasis on the music, and pushed Bono into capturing the essence of the songs by asking him to sing spontaneously. Eno wasn't interested in commercial radio, so the eventual singles "Pride" and "The Unforgettable Fire" were left for Lanois. He was a tech wizard and had everything nailed down for the band to feel free to improvise. At times, the limitations of Slane Castle became too much for him and he'd explode. Equipment breakdowns plagued the recording process, but Kevin Killen, a young engineer, kept things running as smoothly as possible given the limitations.

Larry appreciated Eno and Lanois's bottom-up approach, and was given more time to work on his drumming. Eno was focused on creating textures like the icy arpeggios in "Bad" and the murky soundscape in "A Sort of Homecoming," which Lanois would then fit into more conventional song structures. According to Adam:

> The making of the album was totally different. With Steve [Lillywhite] we were a lot more strict about a song and what it should be; if it did veer off to the right or to the left we would pull it back as opposed to chasing it. Brian and Danny were definitely interested in watching where a song went and chasing it.[6]

One underlying theme running through the album came from the Chicago Peace Museum's exhibition, *The Unforgettable Fire*. It included graphic paintings from the survivors of the Hiroshima and Nagasaki nuclear bombings, which made a lasting impression on Bono. He said:

> It's worth remembering that the Japanese are the only people on earth that really understand the voodoo of $E = mc^2$ and know what it is to have entire cities evaporated.[7]

He was also reading more widely. A few years earlier he had received a book of poetry by Paul Celan, the troubled artist who struggled to reconcile his Jewish faith with the deaths of his family in Auschwitz during World War II. Among his lines was the maxim: "Poetry is a sort of homecoming."[8] These were themes that intrigued Bono, and he connected them to the idea of nonviolent resistance in the face of seemingly insurmountable odds that he was exploring in his readings about Martin Luther King Jr. U2's faith had also become more sophisticated, tempered with the awareness of such twentieth-century atrocities as nuclear war and the Nazi holocaust. Bono said:

> I realized that there *is* a battle, as I see it, between good and evil, and I think you've got to find your place in that. It may be on a factory floor, or it may be in writing songs. It may be trite looking back on it; you know, 'I can't change the world, but I can change a world in me.'[9]

By June they had moved out of Slane Castle and into Windmill Lane for the final touches. Eno had left and Lanois did the final mix of the album. "Pride" was still unfinished and was still causing them a lot of trouble. Then, one day after they returned from lunch, they nailed it in one take.

On July 8, Bob Dylan played a show at Slane Castle and *Hot Press* arranged for Bono to interview him backstage. When Bono arrived he found Dylan in the company of Van Morrison, and the conversation turned to Irish traditional music. Dylan had been introduced to many of the old songs during his time playing in Greenwich Village cafés and listening to the Clancy Brothers in the early sixties. One of U2's favorite Dylan songs, "With God on Our Side" from his 1963 album *The Times They Are A-Changin'*, had even been based on Dominic Behan's Irish ballad, "The Patriot Game." Dylan sang all 11 verses of Brendan Behan's "The Auld Triangle," and scolded Bono for his lack of knowledge about his own country's music. They also discussed Martin Luther King Jr. with Dylan referring to the three kings of Memphis—B. B. King, Elvis, and MLK.[10] Dylan then invited Bono to join him on stage for "Leopard-Skin Pillbox Hat," and Bono ended up adlibbing the lyrics. Dylan was impressed and invited him back to sing on the final song, "Blowin' in the Wind." When Dylan sang the only verses Bono knew, he again made up a new verse on the spot. Bono didn't realize it at the time, but the meeting would have a huge influence on U2 over the next four years.

Expectations were high that *The Unforgettable Fire* would change perceptions about the band and open new doors. They were consciously trying to avoid the provocative aggression that had characterized their sessions with Steve Lillywhite, and subtle evocations were the order of the day. For the cover photo they joined Anton Corbijn on a location search around the Irish countryside and settled on Moydrum, an old, ruined castle near Athlone. For colors they chose scarlet, a break with *War's* black and white, and included a blurry photo of the band. The first taste of this newer, subtler approach was "A Sort of Homecoming." It opens the album with muted percussions rather than the bombastic declarations of *War*, and Edge's playing is wrapped in gauzy silks, not the barbed riffs of "Sunday Bloody Sunday." "Pride (In the Name of Love)," a rousing tribute to Martin Luther King Jr., is the one song on the album that harkens back to their previous sound. Chrissie Hynde, lead singer of the Pretenders, stopped by to add backup vocals. The album also includes genuine amphetamine funk-outs ("Wire"), icy keyboard splashes ("The Unforgettable Fire"), and evocative mood pieces ("4th of July" and "Elvis Presley and America"). The standout track is the torn passion of "Bad." Bono has called it a fusion of Van Morrison and Kraftwerk, and it proved to be a very difficult song to record.[11] A lyric dealing with heroin addiction, "Bad" picks up where "40" left off and joins the list of U2 songs—"With or Without You," "All I Want Is You," "One," "Sometimes You Can't Make It on Your Own"—that begin as smoldering sparks and climax into turbulent infernos. "MLK," written for the album's hero, closes the *The Unforgettable Fire* on a soothing note, revealing U2's newfound interest in gospel.

When *The Unforgettable Fire* was released in October, critics didn't seem to know what to make of it, but it was generally acknowledged as a bold step forward by one of the world's most exciting bands. Liam Mackey in *Hot Press* gave it 12 out of 12, but Robert Hilburn, critic from the *Los Angeles Times,* panned Bono's lyrics as "unnecessarily ethereal and vague."[12]

Around this time, U2 renegotiated their contract with Island Records and secured the copyright to their songs. They turned down bigger offers after realizing the importance of the deal to their future success. In August U2 launched its own label, Mother Records, to promote Irish talent. Their first single was "Coming Thru" by In Tua Nua, which included Vinnie Kilduff, the uilleann pipe player on "Tomorrow," and Steve Wickham, who played violin on "Sunday Bloody Sunday."

At the end of August, U2 left for a month long tour of New Zealand and Australia. They were surprised at how popular they had become and were playing bigger venues than they were used to. One night in Auckland, Bono left the hotel on his own with some fans and went up to a mountain overlooking the city called One Tree Hill, a sacred location for Maori and all New Zealanders alike. As he gazed out on the panoramic view, he was overcome with an expansive sense of freedom and the endless possibilities of the future.[13] At the Auckland show the band met Greg Carroll, a Maori who was working as a stagehand. They were impressed with his work ethic and exuberant personality and hired him for the rest of the tour. He eventually went on to work for U2, becoming Bono's personal assistant. Sadly, he died a few years later in a motorcycle accident, and U2 dedicated a song and their next album to his memory.

Throughout this leg of the tour, U2 was struggling with the new material. They had always needed a few shows to work out the bugs in the new songs, but this time it was taking longer. It was difficult trying to recreate the studio sound, but they didn't want to hire any new members to help out. Necessity is the mother of invention, and Edge soon discovered sequencers as a solution. After they wrapped up in Australia, U2 spent three weeks back in Ireland rehearsing and trying out different arrangements to iron out the problems.

"Pride (In the Name of Love)" was released in September in the UK and then in October in the U.S. as a seven-inch single with "Boomerang II" on the B-side, an instrumental piece Bono had created from a drum machine. In October they kicked off their European tour in France playing smaller venues, but the trimmings—the limos, hotels, and restaurants—were on a much higher level than ever before. U2 was still struggling with the new material, and the damp weather was causing Edge's sequencers to malfunction. To top it off, he was suffering from a cold. Nevertheless, in Belgium, *The Unforgettable Fire* reached number one and the audiences were reacting enthusiastically to the new material. For Larry's twenty-third birthday on Halloween in Rotterdam, Bono sprayed Edge with champagne during the band's performance of "Party Girl." Things were looking up and they were clearly enjoying themselves.

When they returned to the UK, legendary producer Tony Visconti traveled with the band to record live versions for an upcoming album. In Birmingham they captured the version of "Bad" that was later used for the "Wide Awake in America" EP and, two days later at London's Wembley Arena, they recorded the version of "A Sort of Homecoming" that also ended up on the album. A few weeks later, while in Germany, they received an auspicious call from Bob Geldof, the former lead singer of the Boomtown Rats. Bono recalls:

> I didn't know what to make of the call at first, because Bob was Irish, and we looked up to him and respected him, but all I remembered was having rows with Geldof about how he thought pop music and rock 'n' roll should stay away from politics and agitprop, be sexy, fun, mischievous.[14]

Geldof was organizing a one-off supergroup called Band Aid, which would eventually grow into Live Aid, the huge charity concert that took place in the summer of 1985. The BBC had recently run a special TV report on the famine in Ethiopia that was claiming an unprecedented number of lives. It was horrific to see, and it moved Geldof into action. Bono realized the importance of the project and wanted to take part, but he couldn't convince the band to return to London for the recording. Edge had a new family, and Larry had other commitments. Finally, Adam agreed to accompany him. On Sunday, November 25, they arrived in London amid a flurry of preening pop stars. As Bono chilled out with Simon Le Bon from Duran Duran, he looked over the lyrics to "Do They Know It's Christmas," the single Geldof had written with Midge Ure from Ultravox. He liked it, but zeroed in on one sentence he didn't want any part of: "Tonight, thank god, it's them instead of you."[15] It was the most cutting and discomforting line in the song, but he eventually deferred to Geldof and sang it in his best Bruce Springsteen impersonation. Adam didn't sing on any of the verses, but joined in on the star-studded chorus. "Do They Know It's Christmas" shot to number one when it was released on November 29 and stayed at the top of the charts for five weeks. The issue of famine relief became a major topic on the international political agenda, causing a flood of other projects such as USA For Africa's "We Are the World" and Artists United Against Apartheid's "Sun City."

At the beginning of December U2 flew to the U.S. to begin a short two-week tour. From their first show in Philadelphia it become clear they had developed a new approach. Adam strapped on his bass with a wireless transmitter to enable more freedom of movement, Edge carefully laid out his growing collection of effects pedals, and Larry slipped on a headset with a click track. As they started into their set, something was different about Bono, too. The audience was waiting in anticipation for him to mount the speakers, climb the scaffolding or dive into the crowd, but he didn't. As the tour wound on, it became clear that he was making an effort to restrain himself from going as wild as he had on previous tours. He wanted the focus to be on the music, not his exhibitionism. Edge said:

> At this stage, we're trying to let the music speak. You really can't ask him to go on stage and perform like Ian McCulloch, who basically just stands there in front of the microphone and sneers at the crowd. He can't do that—it's not natural for him. But, at the same time, it becomes a problem when people start seeing you as a sort of caricature, a cartoon of yourself.[16]

Audiences still were anxious to see U2 put on the same kind of shows they had seen before. When they played a fund-raiser for Amnesty International's "Stop Torture Week" on December 3 at New York

City's Radio Music Hall, an unexpected scuffle broke out. As U2 took the stage they had barely finished their second song, "I Will Follow," when they stopped to break up a fight in front of the stage. Edge's Explorer fell to the floor, smashing its neck as he rushed to try and restore the peace. The band started up again and made it through the set, but during "Gloria" in the encore they had to stop again. Bono tried to reason with the crowd and they took a ten-minute break while things cooled down. The same problems dogged them in Detroit a week later, and they were becoming rattled. The band wanted to break the "fourth wall" spiritually, not physically, but their fans had other plans. A strange paradox was occurring at U2 shows: though they were celebrating nonviolent figures such as MLK, their music was inspiring the opposite. Somehow their message wasn't getting through. Later that month, U2 made their first visit to the Peace Museum in Chicago to make arrangements for bringing the *Unforgettable Fire* and *Martin Luther King Jr.* exhibits to Dublin in 1985. It was an association the band was eager to encourage and share.

U2 wrapped up their short U.S. tour on December 16 at the Long Beach Arena in California, capping off what had been a tumultuous two weeks. They returned to Ireland for Christmas and then played a three-week tour of Europe in January and February before returning to the United States. U2's popularity had suddenly exploded—their album had begun to make serious inroads all over the country, and their association with "Do They Know It's Christmas?" had significantly increased their profile. The audiences were still excitable and prone to scuffles, but at the larger arenas they were now playing in, things were generally calmer due to the bigger space. Bono still refrained from climbing above the stage and had began using "Amazing Grace" rather than "Send in the Clowns" during "The Electric Co." in case they planned to release it in the future.

On March 1 at the Compton Terrace in Phoenix, an outdoor amphitheater on an Indian reservation, U2 played to 23,000 fans, the largest crowd the band had drawn on its own to that date. The next day in Los Angeles, Bono invited a guitarist from the audience onstage to play Bob Dylan's "Knockin' On Heaven's Door," for the first of what was to become something of a band tradition. Also during this month, *Rolling Stone* crowned U2 "Band of the '80s," and they were now using a Viscount passenger plane to get around the country and living like rock royalty, at least on the road if not at home. In April, U2 sold out New York's Madison Square Garden for the first time ever, and flew over their families and friends from

Dublin to share in the celebration. Two weeks later in Worcester, Massachusetts, U2 sold out three nights in a row. At one show Bono invited a family on stage with a small child. The boy was celebrating a birthday, and Bono gave him his top hat and shared champagne with his parents. April ended with U2 in Atlanta at the Martin Luther King Center after Coretta Scott King, Dr. King's widow, had invited them. Bono's father was flown over to watch the gig that night, and after Bono's introduction, when a spotlight hit him, he flipped his son the finger.[17] Bono was reminded that star power does have its limits, especially when it comes to family.

After the tour finished, U2 released a four-song EP with the misleading title *Wide Awake in America*—misleading because the two live songs, "A Sort of Homecoming" and "Bad," were actually recorded in the UK. It also contained two outtakes from *The Unforgettable Fire* sessions, "The Three Sunrises" and "Love Comes Tumbling," and sold surprisingly well with the eight-minute version of "Bad" receiving heavy radio airplay. *The Unforgettable Fire* had sold in higher numbers than any of their previous albums. "Pride" spent 15 weeks on the single charts, peaking at number 33, U2's highest showing at the time, but it still didn't crack the top 20. It was released too early in the tour for it to get the attention it deserved. College radio picked up "A Sort of Homecoming" and "Wire," helping to propel the album to over one million copies—their first platinum record in the United States.

At the end of June, U2 played a "Homecoming Concert" at Dublin's Croke Park with REM and the Alarm. In front of 57,000 fans, it felt like a victory celebration: they were at the top of the charts and had finally broken into the United States. It was the first time they performed "Sunday Bloody Sunday" in the same location where the 1920 massacre of the song's title took place. For their encore they played an impromptu version of Bruce Springsteen's "My Hometown."

Bob Geldof had called U2 again, asking them to play the upcoming Live Aid concert at Wembley Stadium on July 13. The band knew it was going to be huge and were excited, but they were also terrified. Each performer was given only 20 minutes, and U2 was scheduled for late in the afternoon. The night before, they called Geldof to say that without a sound check they didn't want to perform. He brushed off their concerns, assuring them everything would work out.[18] On the day of the concert, the backstage area was a circus with technicians, engineers, and camera people running around amid the big name stars that Geldof had assembled. U2 mingled with David Bowie, Paul McCartney, Freddie Mercury, and even Muhammad Ali.

Two concerts were taking place simultaneously: one in London's Wembley Stadium, the other at JFK Stadium in Philadelphia. After Brian Adams finished in Philadelphia, Jack Nicholson introduced U2 and sent the satellite back as U2 took the stage at 5:20 London time. They had decided to perform three songs: "Sunday Bloody Sunday," "Bad," and "Pride." Dressed in a black riding coat, leather pants tucked into suede boots, and a white dress shirt adorned with a western bolo tie, Bono gazed out on the 88,000 gathered that afternoon looking every bit the Romantic idealist he had been aspiring to embody. As he brushed back his mane of hair, letting it fall over his shoulders, he could see fans waving the Irish tricolor alongside a few white U2 flags. He looked a bit jittery, as though he had been wired into an electric socket.

"Sunday Bloody Sunday" kicked things off, and Bono soon redirected a cameraman away from the band toward the audience while leading them in a chorus of "No more! No more!" "Bad" continued the liftoff. After shouting, "Fade away . . . No!" Bono suddenly dropped his mic and began scanning the front row for someone to bring up on stage. The rest of the band lost sight of him as he flipped himself over the barrier at the front and began pointing to two women. A group of yellow-shirted security guards swarmed around one young woman and pulled her over the barrier. Bono embraced her, swaying to the fluttering arpeggios the band had been playing in steady rotation as over one billion around the world watched on in amazement. Bono then climbed back on stage where two other women were waiting for him. He gave them a swift kiss before taking the mic from his personal assistant Greg Carroll to finish off "Bad" with snippets from Lou Reed's "Satellite of Love" and "Walk on the Wild Side" mashed in with "Ruby Tuesday" and "Sympathy for the Devil" by the Rolling Stones. He then dropped the mic again, waved to the crowd and walked off stage. Altogether they played their allotted 20 minutes with "Bad" lasting over 12 minutes. Edge recalls:

He was gone for so long I started to think maybe he had decided to end the set early and was on his way to the dressing room. I'm glad the cameras didn't show the rest of the band during the whole drama, because we must have looked like the Three Stooges up there: Curly, Larry and Moe.[19]

It had been a breathtaking spectacle, but the band was furious with Bono and afterward there was a heated argument. Everyone, including Bono, was convinced that the set had been a disaster. They packed everything up and returned to Ireland. Bono was feeling depressed and went with Ali to her parents' home in Wexford. While there, he met a sculptor in his sixties who had seen the show on TV and had been inspired to create a work he called "The Leap" based on Bono's performance.[20] It was the first sign that things hadn't gone so badly after all. The day after the show, all the reports were about how U2, and Bono in particular, had been one of the major highlights of the show. His embrace of the fans symbolized the humanity of the event, and all of U2's albums entered the charts again around the world. U2 issued a statement to the UK press asking, "Are we part of a civilization that protects itself by investing in life . . . or investing in death?"[21] In the end, Bono's performance became one of the iconic moments of the 1980s. As Adam said:

> Bono's journey really meant something, it carried the emotion of the day to people. So his performer's instinct was right. Again.[22]

After Live Aid, the band took a break. In August, Amnesty International's U.S. Director, Jack Healey, visited Paul in Dublin to ask if U2 would participate in a tour the next year to raise awareness about human rights and Amnesty's efforts to stop their abuse. Paul recognized it was exactly the thing U2 should do and committed the band. Bono also got a call from Little Steven Van Zandt, the guitarist from Bruce Springsteen's E Street Band. The pop world was experiencing a renaissance of political awareness, and Little Steven had just written a song to address apartheid in South Africa. He had asked some of the biggest stars of the day to play on it, including Springsteen, Miles Davis, and Bob Dylan. Bono didn't need much convincing and, in August, he recorded his part for Artists United Against Apartheid's "Sun City" in Dublin. At the end of the month, U2 made a surprise appearance at the Lark by the Lee Festival in Cork. Edge was also keeping busy working on a soundtrack with Canadian producer and friend Michael Brook for a film called *Captive* starring

Oliver Reed. For the single, "Heroine," he enlisted a young singer from Dublin, Sinead O'Connor, to sing lead vocals.

In September, Bono and Ali traveled to Ethiopia to volunteer in a feeding station in Ajibar for five weeks. Together they helped promote health, hygiene, and basic farming methods by staging one-act plays and writing songs to perform. At one point a man offered Bono his child, saying if he stayed in Ethiopia he would surely die. Bono had to say no, but it left an indelible impression he never forgot. Bono documented the entire experience with a series of photos that he later assembled into a book called *String of Pearls.*

On his first day back from Africa Bono jumped on the first plane to New York to take part in the "Sun City" video. While there, he met up with his friend, the J. Geils vocalist from the 1982 tour, Peter Wolf. The pair went to visit the Rolling Stones in the studio where they were recording *Dirty Work* with Steve Lillywhite. Bono hit it off with Mick Jagger and Keith Richards, who shared old blues and country standards with him late into the night. After returning to his hotel room, Bono was feeling exhilarated and couldn't sleep—he wrote "Silver and Gold" instead. The next day he contacted Keith Richards, who invited him back to the studio. With Ron Wood on slide, Richards on rhythm, and Bono on vocals, they cut the track. When Little Steven heard the track's anguished blues, he immediately wanted it on the *Sun City* EP. It was too late to list on the sleeve credits, so the album was released with a sticker announcing the song's inclusion.

Bono returned to Ireland and, in December, went into the studio with the Irish band Clannad. He had been interested in transforming traditional Irish music into a more contemporary style, and Clannad was one band that was doing just that. U2 had used Clannad's haunting, "Harry's Game" as exit music during *The Unforgettable Fire* tour. In January 1986, a duet between Bono and singer Maire Brennan, "In A Lifetime," was released from Clannad's album *Macalla.* The video was shot the month before in Gweedore, a small town in Donegal, Ireland. At the end of January, U2 surfaced on an RTÉ show called TV Gaga with Edge looking like a French artist in a beret and ponytail and Bono sporting a bandana and a Harley-Davidson T-shirt. They answered a few questions and performed a shambolic song called "Woman Fish" and an early version of "Trip through Your Wires." The first issue of *Propaganda,* U2's fanclub magazine, also debuted this month.

In early 1986, U2 began rehearsing songs for their next album in Adam's home at Danesmoate in the south of Dublin. They decided they would stay with the production team of Brian Eno and Danny Lanois, believing they would improve on their sound and chart new directions. As U2 were settling into the recording, the time came for the Amnesty International tour, beginning in June. It was the human rights organization's twenty-fifth anniversary and they had assembled a number of acts, including Lou Reed, Peter Gabriel, and a reunited Police for their Conspiracy of Hope tour. U2 knew it would push back the release of their next album, but were convinced it was worth it.

Just before leaving on the tour, U2 played Self Aid in May, a 14-hour charity show for Dublin's unemployed with Van Morrison, Clannad, and a host of other Irish acts. U2 revealed a new look: "peasant chic." The look featured long hair, scruffy beards, and fringe jackets. They played a six-song set that included Eddie Cochran's "C'mon Everybody," Bob Dylan's "Maggie's Farm," and John Lennon's "Cold Turkey." The concert came in for some harsh criticism. The Irish magazine *In Dublin* ran a cover story, "The Great Self-Aid Farce—Rock Against the People," accusing U2 of hypocrisy and predicting the concert would allow the government to further neglect its responsibilities. Bono responded by including the lyrics, "They crawled out of the woodwork / Onto the pages of cheap Dublin magazines," into "Bad" during their concert performance.[23]

The Conspiracy of Hope tour kicked off in San Francisco on June 4 with U2 closing some of the shows and Bono joining the reunited Police on their song, "Invisible Sun." The tour culminated in an 11-hour concert in front of 55,000 fans at New York's Giants Stadium on June 15. At the end, the Police took off their instruments and gave them to U2 as a symbolic passing of the torch. The tour accelerated U2's popularity in North America and cemented their image as the only band of the 1980s that truly mattered.

NOTES

1. Alan, 88.
2. *U2 by U2*, 148.
3. Alan, 87.
4. *The Making of the Unforgettable Fire*, http://www.youtube.com/watch?v=KLoC1F8WSHY (accessed April 29, 2009).

5. *U2 by U2,* 151.
6. Alan, 89.
7. *U2 by U2,* 152.
8. "Quest For Fire." November 16, 1984. www.hotpress.com: http://www.hotpress.com/archive/549247.html (accessed April 29, 2009).
9. Rolling Stone, 35.
10. *U2 by U2,* 155.
11. Ibid., 157.
12. Alan, 90.
13. McGee, 78.
14. *U2 by U2,* 157.
15. Ibid., 158.
16. Alan, 101.
17. McGee, 86.
18. Ibid., 88.
19. *U2 by U2,* 162.
20. Ibid., 164.
21. McGee, 89.
22. *U2 by U2,* 164.
23. McGee, 94.

CHAPTER FIVE

Rattled & Hummed: *The Joshua Tree* & International Stardom (1986–1990)

The Conspiracy of Hope Tour had a huge impact on the individual members of U2 in a way that no other tour had. They felt part of a collective fighting for the rights of the dispossessed while building a mass movement through each concert. The tour raised Amnesty International's profile significantly in the United States; the human rights group raised over US$3 million.[1]

In July, tragedy struck. Greg Carroll, Bono's personal assistant, died suddenly in a motorcycle accident in Dublin. A few weeks after the Amnesty tour finished, Bono had arrived in Texas for the Farm Aid II concert when he got a call that Greg had died. Bono, Ali, Larry, and his girlfriend, Ann, flew to New Zealand where Greg was given a traditional Maori burial. His passing profoundly affected Bono, who regarded Greg as a brother, and added a deeper sense of purpose to his work on the new album. After the burial, Bono and Ali flew to Nicaragua on the invitation of Central American Mission Partners (CAMP), a group dedicated to human rights and aiding peasant farmers in Nicaragua and El Salvador. Bono had met one of the group's leaders, David Batstone, through San Francisco's Glide Memorial United Methodist Church during the Amnesty tour, and was inspired to visit the region.[2,3] During this period President Ronald Reagan was conducting a covert war using the Contras against the Sandinista government of Nicaragua and the FMLN rebels in El Salvador. Bono recalls:

> I had an extraordinary time in Nicaragua, and fell in love with this very musical, very cultural place. The ideas of the revolution were, from my point of view, a coming together of many of my interests: Christianity, social justice, artists in power.[4]

While there, Bono and Ali met with Ernesto Cardenal, a Roman Catholic priest, poet, and, at the time, minister of culture. On one occasion they attended a speech by President Daniel Ortega without knowing author Salman Rushdie was also in the crowd. They then traveled to El Salvador and met a group called COMADRES—the Mothers of the Disappeared. One day, while delivering aid to farmers about 100 miles north of San Salvador their entourage came under fire from government forces.[5] They witnessed some villages sympathetic to the rebels completely wiped out and others suffering huge fatalities. These events haunted Bono, making an indelible impression that would help shape his vision for the next album.

When Bono returned to Dublin he was in dire need of some rest and relaxation. He hooked up with his old friends Gavin and Guggi and began enjoying himself in a way that he hadn't for a long time, going out to clubs and listening to local music. U2's rise to fame had kept them apart, and now they could rekindle old relationships. Edge had a new daughter, Arran, and was delving deeper into American music and film. While touring across the United States, U2 had been struck by the wide-open panorama of the American landscape and they were falling in love with its mythology. This would contribute to the new album's theme—the beauty and romance of the "American Dream" versus the crass barbarity and greed of U.S. foreign policy.

U2 started rehearsing at Danesmoate, Adam's home studio, with a new engineer, Mark Ellis, also known as Flood. He had worked with New Order and Nick Cave and the Bad Seeds and had already been active in the London underground scene. Flood's involvement guaranteed U2's desire to maximize the studio's potential would continue. Guggi and Gavin started hanging out in the upper floors of the house, painting with Bono once in a while. They would occasionally listen in on the sessions and provide valuable feedback.[6] In the middle of the rehearsals, Daniel Lanois showed up with Robbie Robertson from the legendary group, The Band. Lanois was producing

Robertson's first solo album, and U2 enthusiastically agreed to work on two tracks, "Sweet Fire of Love" and "Testimony." This continued U2's ongoing exploration of American music. Robertson would eventually return the favor and narrate a documentary on the making of U2's future film, *Rattle and Hum.* In October, U2 attended a B. B. King show in Dublin and met backstage with the veteran blues troubadour, who would record "When Love Comes to Town" with the band a few years later.

Lanois and Eno briefly joined U2 at Danesmoate, then moved over to Windmill Lane Studios. As it always is with U2, the recording process was arduous and painstakingly slow. It was the fall of 1986 and the music charts were stuffed with bland, middle-of-the-road music by aging pop stars like Michael McDonald and Peter Cetera, or poodle rockers like Bon Jovi. U2 was determined to shake things up with the new album, but they decided it would be less experimental than *The Unforgettable Fire* and they delivered on both counts. The sweeping opener, "Where the Streets Have No Name," rises slowly into the mix like the sun burning away storm clouds, heralding the beginning of what was to become one of U2's greatest albums. It was such a difficult song to record that at one point Eno got so sick of it he almost erased it from the master tapes.

The advice Bob Dylan gave to Bono in the summer of 1984 about going back to the roots of music had made a huge impact, and its influence was turning up in everything U2 was doing. Touring the United States over the previous six years compounded Dylan's words and spurred their interest in American blues and R&B. "I Still Haven't Found What I'm Looking For" began as a blues number under the working title "Under The Weather Girls." It sounded like a lame reggae tune until it came time for Bono to find a melody line. While at the mic, he suddenly began singing a stirring gospel melody as Edge handed him a title idea he had written down on a scrap of paper earlier that day.[7] Bono sang it and the rest is history.

Another big breakthrough occurred when Bono came up with the chord progression to "With or Without You." The band began playing around with the dynamics, building it up and bringing it back down again. Edge had just received an "Infinite guitar," an invention by friend Michael Brook that gave him the ability to sustain a note, similar to a violin. While Edge was experimenting, Bono seized on the sound as the missing ingredient the song needed.[8] "With or Without You" reflects the tension Bono was feeling between his responsibilities as an artist and as a husband. He envied singers like Shane MacGowan from the Pogues, who did whatever he wanted in pursuit of his muse no matter what the consequences. So deep was his admiration, that a decade later Bono appeared in a BBC2 documentary called *The Great Hunger—The Life and Songs of Shane MacGowan*, in which he referred to MacGowan as "the greatest songwriter Ireland has ever produced."[9] Bono was worried his married life was dulling the resonance of his art.[10] He was caught in a trap, realizing he couldn't live "with or without" Ali or his other love—music.

"Bullet the Blue Sky" came together early in the sessions as Bono was internalizing the horror he had witnessed in Central America. Liberation theology was emerging as an influential form of Christianity at the time, and it inspired Bono:

> I think the danger of liberation theology is that it can become a very *material* ethic, too material. But I am really inspired by it. If you're not committed to the poor, what is religion? It's a black hole.[11]

He was convinced Ronald Reagan's foreign policy was to blame for the suffering he had seen, and felt compelled to address it. He hounded Edge to put the sound of the war—the fighter planes, bombs, and bullets—through his amp to make it "feel like hell on earth."[12] Edge emulated Jimi Hendrix by using feedback to capture the fevered paranoia of being trapped in a war zone.

While U2 was recording in January 1986, friend and mentor Phil Lynott from Thin Lizzy died of a heroin overdose. "Running to Stand Still" revisited the issue though the eyes of a couple of addicts living in the "seven towers," or the high-rise complex of Ballymun near where Bono had grown up. Bono was feeling more confident as a lyricist than he ever had before, and was becoming aware of the poetic power of his lyrics. He was reading widely, particularly American writers like Flannery O'Connor, Charles Bukowski, and Allen Ginsberg, and the song's nonjudgmental tone revealed these new influences.

In the middle of the sessions Bono became concerned the album was lacking faster songs. At one point he strapped on a guitar and banged out a chord progression to push Edge into playing some more up-tempo rock numbers. "In God's Country" and "Trip Through Your Wires" were the result. "One Tree Hill," both a tribute and a lament for Greg Carroll, was such a personal song for Bono that he couldn't bear to listen to it or handle any criticism about his delivery.[13] When the album was finally released it was dedicated to Greg. "Exit," the darkest song in U2's repertoire up to that point, signaled a new maturity and a willingness to tackle more challenging material. During the Amnesty tour, in addition to the Salvadoran women from COMADRES, Bono also had met some of the mothers who had lost loved ones under General Pinochet's regime in Chile. He later wrote "Mothers of the Disappeared" on classical guitar for them.

Paul was concerned the band was taking too long getting the final album together, and he called Steve Lillywhite in to help. He thought Eno and Lanois were the craftsmen, but lacked the "pop ears" to get a radio hit. Lillywhite had had success getting U2 songs on the radio, and he ended up mixing four tracks—"Where the Streets Have No Name," "With or Without You," "Bullet the Blue Sky," and "Red Hill Mining Town." At the time he was married to the now-deceased singer Kirsty MacColl and she was given the privilege of deciding the order of the songs, starting with the ones she liked the best. Her only instruction was the first song should be "Where the Streets Have No Name," and the last, "Mothers of the Disappeared."[14]

The idea for the cover came from a theme that had developed during the recording process—spiritual thirst and yearning. The band agreed the desert would be an ideal setting to symbolize this concept, and in mid-December they joined Anton Corbijn out in the Mojave Desert and Death Valley east of Los Angeles. They spent a couple of days staying in motels and driving around to various locations on a bus. They noticed lots of twisted cacti, called Joshua trees, dotting the landscape. Early settlers thought their gnarled branches conjured up the Old Testament prophet Joshua pointing the way to the promised land. Bono liked the name and the symbolism. Larry later said U2 never went in search of *The Joshua Tree*—it came looking for them.[15] The album cover was shot at Zabriskie Point in Death Valley with the band resembling early settlers or pilgrims. The surrounding landscape conjures up a Biblical scene not unlike something from the Sinai desert in Egypt.

When *The Joshua Tree* was released March 9, it shot to number one in almost every country. Eventually it became the first-ever platinum CD, selling over one million copies on disc alone in the United States. It also became the fastest-selling album in British music history, selling 300,000 copies in its first two days. *The Joshua Tree* was a triumph, and U2 was living up to their plan to be the best band of the decade.

They arrived in the United States in late March to do publicity and rehearse for the upcoming tour and began filming a documentary for MTV with Meiert Avis and Barry Devlin called *Outside It's America*. The video for "Where the Streets Have No Name" was filmed at the end of the month and performed on the rooftop of a liquor store in Los Angeles. The band performed the song four separate times, along with "Pride," "In God's Country," "Sunday Bloody Sunday," and a cover of Curtis Mayfield's "People Get Ready." The police finally had to order U2 to shut down due to fears the crowd was getting out of hand, but the video went on to a win a Grammy for Best Music Video and remains a fan favorite.

The tour opened soon after on April 2 in Tempe, Arizona, and all the signs suggested *The Joshua Tree* was going to be a blockbuster. But when U2 arrived for their first show they had no idea they were walking into a controversy involving Martin Luther King Jr. The governor of Arizona, Evan Mecham, had repealed the state's January holiday for King's birthday, and a large grassroots opposition movement had grown to recall him. At least two acts had cancelled shows—the Doobie Brothers and Stevie Wonder—and the pressure was on U2 to do something. They were prepared to cancel the shows if necessary, but after talking with both fans and with members of a statewide campaign to recall Mecham, they decided to go ahead with the concert as a way of dramatizing opposition to the governor's decision. Bono condemned the move in an interview and drew fire from the governor's office. U2 then made a substantial cash donation to a watchdog committee monitoring the governor.

At the opening of the show tensions were high in anticipation of what might happen. Promoter Barry Fey read out a statement by U2 expressing the band's outrage and condemning the repeal of the King holiday. U2 then took the stage to the hymn-like opening of "Where the Streets Have No Name," with the crowd roaring its approval. After the first few songs Bono began losing his voice, as had happened at previous opening shows, but the audience rallied to his support and filled in the lyrics he couldn't pull off, including the new material. By the end, Bono's voice was shot, but the band picked up the slack and played even harder to make up for the shortcoming. It paid off—reviews of the show were good and word of mouth spread about U2's undiminished intensity. A year later Mecham was impeached; King's holiday was eventually defeated by a referendum in 1990, only to be reinstated in 1992.

The shows of this first leg were unforgettable, especially Edge's heavy guitar work on "Bullet the Blue Sky." He said:

I'm getting into rock and roll again. I mean, obviously, our style—but with the basic ingredients of rock and roll: guitar, backbeat, bass, drums, vocal. No messing about. That's where I'm sort of leaning now—the direction of the band.[16]

Their sets included "Still Haven't Found What I'm Looking For," "Running to Stand Still," "With or Without You," Pride," "Sunday Bloody Sunday," "Gloria," and "I Will Follow." Their choice of covers such as Curtis Mayfield's "People Get Ready," Neil Young's "Southern Man," and Dylan's "I Shall Be Released" revealed their ongoing interest in the blues, R&B, and iconic rockers from the 1960s. Bono and Edge looked the part of long-haired hippies with their wide-brimmed hats, ponytails, and Peruvian vests, while Adam and Larry kept things more austere and simple.

This focus on the past, the 1960s in particular, struck some as a reaction to the more contemporary sound of *The Unforgettable Fire,* but this failed to take into account the actual music of *The Joshua Tree.* It captured the spirit of the times by using the gloss of the era to subvert its hollow core. The production is state of the art, seamless and so smooth it glistens, but the contents are as raw as a serrated limb. Much of *The Joshua Tree*—"Bullet the Blue Sky," "Mothers of the Disappeared," and "Exit"—are portraits of the American dream gone rancid, while the rest of the album conveys pain, loss, and yearning. But the album never sinks under the weight of its heavy themes—something intrinsic within the band, call it hope, faith or magic—propels the songs and the listener upward, where any suffering is ultimately overcome. Whereas the physical trappings and their choice of cover songs may have suggested a previous time, U2's music was as relevant as anything by their peers, if not much more so. For the first time, Bono was feeling proud of his lyrics. Up to that point he had left them to the last minute, even writing them at the mic in his own personal dialect the band termed "Bongelese."[17] With *The Joshua Tree* he had taken ownership of the words and was emerging as a genuine craftsman, if not an actual poet.

During a break between shows, U2 flew to Las Vegas to watch Sugar Ray Leonard and Marvin Hagler in a boxing match. They then attended a Frank Sinatra show at the Golden Nugget and joined him backstage after the show. A week later, after their second concert in

Houston, they took over a local bar called the LA Club for an after-show party. Paul made an arrangement with the club manager to close the doors once the band arrived. U2 began mingling and enjoying the live country music and eventually took the stage with some backing from a few musicians in the house band. They played a short set that included Johnny Cash's "I Walk the Line" and "Folsom Prison Blues," as well as "Lost Highway," the song popularized by Hank Williams Sr., and a stripped-down version of "I Still Haven't Found What I'm Looking For." For those lucky enough to be there, it was a rare opportunity to see U2 having fun in an intimate setting, free from the celebrity cage that was too often leaving them feeling isolated. The band was still learning about American roots music. During the tour, Bono asked Peter Wolf for a mixed tape of classic country and western songs, and Boston DJ Carter Allan presented him with an Atlantic Records box set of vintage blues cassettes.[18]

At the beginning of the shows, U2 would follow backing band Lone Justice and take the stage while the lights were still on. With John's Lennon's version of Ben E. King's "Stand by Me" still playing, first Larry would slip behind the drums, followed by Adam and Edge, until Bono finally took over the vocals as the canned music faded out. Most of the time the audience didn't realize what was happening until it was only U2 left playing onstage. For the California shows U2 was joined by Bob Dylan in Los Angeles on "I Shall Be Released" and "Knockin' on Heaven's Door." After the show Bono told Dylan his songs would last forever. Dylan replied, "Your songs are gonna last forever too—the only thing is, no one's gonna be able to play them."[19] It was a huge thrill to play with Dylan, and after the show they joined him and T-Bone Burnett in Edge's room at the Sunset Marquis for a few drinks. They started writing a song together, and Dylan floored Bono and Edge. He was coming up with some amazing verses in what seemed like an effortless manner.

They were beginning to realize that their fame wasn't bringing them the satisfaction they thought it would. On top of it, the pressures of touring were taking their toll on Edge and his young family. Despite the price it was exacting from their personal lives, the tour was a huge financial success. U2 was easily selling out 15,000 seat arenas, and *The Joshua Tree* had hit Billboard's number one within four weeks of its release. Both *Newsweek* and *Time* magazines had features on the band, with the latter including the cover story headline "Rock's Hottest Ticket." By the beginning of May, "With or Without You" made number one, and U2 released "I Still Haven't

Found What I'm Looking For" with "Spanish Eyes" and "Deep in the Heart" as B-sides.

After the tour wrapped up in the middle of May, U2 went back to Dublin where they expressed some regrets over how their new star status was alienating them from their audience and attracting a different type of fan. The press was also questioning whether they could still claim to be able to speak for those less fortunate when they were making millions of dollars. The early stresses of success were beginning to show. As Bono said, the band was developing an image of po-faced young men who seemed too stupid to enjoy their success.[20]

The European tour kicked off on May 27 in Rome. Their next single, "I Still Haven't Found What I'm Looking For," was released in June, and it too went to number one, becoming one of the biggest hits of the 1987 summer. Barry Devlin had filmed the video earlier in Las Vegas with the band walking down the strip mingling with surprised fans. U2 was playing to huge crowds in Madrid, Munich, Paris, and Wembley Arena in London. The night before the London shows, Bono had been listening repeatedly to Roy Orbison's 1963 single "In Dreams," which had been featured prominently in David Lynch's 1986 cult film, *Blue Velvet.* The next morning Bono began writing "She's a Mystery to Me," and sang it to the band. At the gig later that day the band received a message that Roy Orbison wanted to meet them. They were all shocked and marveled at the coincidence; Bono and Orbison agreed to work together later in the year.[21]

A few days later, in Glasgow, U2 recorded a live version of Phil Spector and Darlene Love's "Christmas (Baby, Please Come Home)" for Jimmy Iovine's upcoming charity album *A Very Special Christmas.* They then played Cork, Ireland, on August 8, Edge's birthday, before taking a month off. Paul began filling in the details for filming U2's upcoming return tour through the United States, but he wasn't sure how to go about it exactly. Bono and Ali used the break to return to the Greenbelt Christian Festival disguised as stewards to avoid attention. They spent time with ministers John Smith from Australia and Gustavo Parajon from Nicaragua and Canadian musician Bruce Cockburn.[22]

In September, U2 returned to the United States for a three-and-a-half month tour, moving into stadiums with crowds of up to 50,000. They had also decided on a 27-year-old filmmaker, Phil Joanou, to film a rockumentary. He didn't have much experience, but he was a protégé of Stephen Spielberg and a passionate U2 fan. Everything was falling into place, and the band had reached another level—they were no longer the underdogs, but the stars. They had sold millions of records and were using their fame to shine a light on issues of social justice; they believed that rock 'n' roll could make human rights more relevant for their audiences. U2 actively supported Amnesty International, and allowed the charity to set up booths at their concerts.

When they played RFK Stadium in Washington, D.C., Bono slipped and dislocated his shoulder while singing "Exit." He finished the concert and then went straight to the hospital. Joanou hopped in the ambulance to film the entire scene, but it never made it into the film, and Bono stayed in a sling for close to a month. In Philadelphia, Bruce Springsteen joined the band onstage in front of a huge crowd of 86,000 fans for a version of "Stand by Me." U2 was at the height of their popularity, and opportunities were plentiful. The band got word about a gospel choir called the New Voices of Freedom from the Greater Calvary Baptist Church in Harlem that had reworked "I Still Haven't Found What I'm Looking For" into a spiritual. U2 went to visit and was so impressed that they invited the choir onstage at their upcoming Madison Square Garden show at the end of September. While walking around the neighborhood they bumped into two buskers, Adam Gussow and Sterling Magee, performing "Freedom for My People," which they later included in the film and album, *Rattle And Hum*.

For the eastern leg of the tour they rented houses in the Hamptons in New York state, and they flew back after each show. It was a cold fall and the band felt isolated and bored. They released "Where the Streets Have No Name" as the third single, and it made it to number 13 in November. At some of the shows the band was dressing up in wigs to perform a short opening spot as the Dalton Brothers— Betty, Alton, Luke, and Duke. Adam slipped into a dress as Betty Dalton, and they played some of the country songs they had played at the Houston club the previous spring. It was a fun diversion that deflated the pomp and circumstance surrounding their official role as U2, and foreshadowed some of the kitsch that was to come in the early 1990s during their Zoo TV tour.

During these shows, Phil Joanou, "ET" as the band had nicknamed him for the size of his head, was running around trying to capture the best film footage of the band. In Denver on November 8, the day of the Remembrance Day bombing in Enniskillen, Northern Ireland, Bono delivered a blistering condemnation of the perpetrators, saying at one point, "F*** Freedom!" It later made its way into the film. Three days later, in San Francisco, the band put on a free, out-door "Save the Yuppies" concert at the Justin Herman Plaza. They chose to open with Bob Dylan's "All Along the Watchtower" and were rehearsing it in their trailer minutes before going on stage. While performing it, Bono spray-painted "Rock N Roll Stops Traffic" on the Vaillancourt Fountain next to the stage, and later had to issue a written apology to Mayor Diane Feinstein for the "vandalism." During "Sunday Bloody Sunday," Bono mistook a "SF" flag for Sinn Féin, the political wing of the IRA. Forgetting he was in San Francisco he began ranting against the violence in Northern Ireland, singling out the Enniskillen bombing that had recently occurred. It was a startling glimpse of the anger Bono reserved for anyone who attempted to romanticize "the troubles" of U2's native land. A few days later, while performing across the bay in Oakland, U2 invited Armand Vaillancourt, the Quebecois designer of the fountain, to come onstage and even the score. Vaillancourt expressed solidarity with U2 and spray-painted "Stop The Madness" on their stage.[23]

A week later, Bono woke up in Los Angeles with a song already written in his head. He had been dreaming of Bob Dylan and thought it might actually belong to him, so he called him up and Dylan invited him out to his place in Malibu. Together they worked on a version of what was to become "Love Rescue Me," agreeing to record it together. Edge was also writing new material and putting sketches together for "Desire" and "All I Want Is You." Bono wrote "When Love Comes to Town" for B. B. King, who was opening for the band at some of their shows. The song blew King away, and he told Bono the lyrics were very heavy for someone of his age to write.

When U2 was in Memphis they visited Elvis's Graceland home, and a few hours later popped up at Sun Studios with Cowboy Jack Clement, the original engineer on Elvis's first records. He pulled out some old equipment that hadn't been used since the 1960s, as well as mics that Elvis had recorded with. The band could hardly believe their luck—here were a bunch of Irish lads inside the inner sanctuary where some of the very first rock 'n' roll songs had been made with legends Elvis, Johnny Cash, Carl Perkins, and Jerry Lee Lewis. They made the most of the opportunity and cut "When Love Comes to Town" and another new song written for Billie Holiday, "Angel Of Harlem," with the famed Memphis Horns. At this point, it wasn't clear they were making a double album, but they knew the songs were to be used on an upcoming release to accompany the film.

The Joshua Tree tour finally wrapped up on December 20 where it had started nine months earlier, in Tempe, Arizona. It had changed their lives, transforming U2 into international stars in the same league as Madonna or Michael Jackson. They returned to Dublin, leaving the film editing with Joanou in Los Angeles. Paramount Pictures offered to finance it with the plan to open it in over 100 theaters. Joanou was left with 150 hours of footage, and eventually needed to fly to Dublin in May 1988 to do some extra interviews with the band to help the film's narrative structure.

In Dublin, U2 was continuing to work on the songs they had sketched out for what they now decided was going to be a double album. "Desire" started coming together based on "1969," the Stooges' version of the Bo Diddley beat. In January, Bono joined an exhibition in Dublin with Gavin and Guggi with his Ethiopian photos titled *A String of Pearls* after his book of the same name. Soon after this, U2 relocated to Los Angeles to finish work on *Rattle and Hum*, now the confirmed name for the new album and the film; the title was taken from a lyric in "Bullet the Blue Sky." Rather than simply do another live album, they were determined to make it a special combination of live and new studio songs and chose Jimmy Iovine, who had worked on *Under a Blood Red Sky*, to produce it. They found a huge, old house in Bel Air and began to have some fun soaking up the LA lifestyle. Bono did a lot of partying, and Adam even visited the Playboy Mansion. Edge was in LA with his family, and resisted the temptations while holding it together with Iovine in the studio. Larry missed Dublin, and spent most of his down time riding Harleys around LA.

At the Grammy Awards in March, *The Joshua Tree* beat out Michael Jackson's *Bad* to win both Album of the Year and Best Rock Performance. When asked about U2's mainstream commercial success, Bono responded with a sly grin, "We're slipstream, not mainstream." The next day Jackson invited U2 backstage at Madison Square Garden for a visit, but when they realized his personal cameraman was filming them they left as soon as possible.[24] Back in LA they continued recording, and "All I Want Is You," with lyrics written for Ali, emerged as an epic, sweeping song. Legendary producer and arranger Van Dyke Parks was invited to add some strings, and ended up writing a two-and-a-half minute coda. Iovine's style was to critique the material and leave the band alone to find their own way. He wasn't a musician who could play along and collaborate, and this didn't suit U2 as well as they had hoped. They really needed someone like Eno or Lanois to offer new material as incentives to make better songs.

U2 returned to Dublin in May and continued recording at the Point Depot Theater. Joanou came over and filmed some scenes, including the band running through "Desire." The next month U2 was back in LA recording "Hawkmoon 269" at Sunset Studios amid the chaos of Hollywood, with Bob Dylan dropping by to play organ. While reading Albert Goldman's scathing biography, *The Lives of John Lennon,* Bono wrote the lyrics to "God Part II," after Lennon's song on his 1970 solo debut. Ironically, it contained the ultimate critique of what U2 was doing: glorifying the past "when the future dries up." In the middle of the sessions, U2 was invited to participate in a charity recording of Woody Guthrie and Huddie "Leadbelly" Ledbetter songs, with the proceeds going to the Smithsonian Institute. They chose Guthrie's "Jesus Christ," recorded the previous December at Sun Studios, done with a "hallelujah" chorus. In a promotional video for the album, Bono explained:

> There's a lie that's very popular right now, which is you can't make a difference, you can't change our world. A lot of songs on the radio perpetuate that lie, for me. They have words, but they don't mean anything, they have a melody but the music sounds the same. It's the same song and it puts people in this big sleep. I think Woody Guthrie's music was much more . . . awake than that.[25]

The new album was meant to be a scrapbook of U2's U.S. tour, but they realized near the end of the recording that they wouldn't be able to get away with it. The songs were too conventional and overwrought. The band had become lazy, burnt out, and had shied away from challenging themselves. The film was almost finished, and the band was being asked for its approval on everything. Joanou's perspective had been sacrificed, and it was becoming too self-conscious and reverential. Nevertheless, Paramount put a huge ad campaign behind it and expectations were very high. "Desire" was released in early September and made it to number three on Billboard. *Rattle and Hum,* the album, was released first on October 5, and as it shot to number one the film followed the next month. The album's 17 songs included 8 live tracks from *The Joshua Tree* tour and 9 studio recordings. It was awash in American icons, from Billie Holiday and B. B. King to Bob Dylan and Jimi Hendrix, and the band found they had to defend themselves by saying they were fans of these legends, not their equals. Both releases received harsh criticism; U2 was accused of appropriating American music without creating anything original.

Just before the film opened around the world, U2 played the benefit concert *Smile Jamaica* in London, and Keith Richards joined them on "When Love Comes to Town." *Rattle And Hum* the film opened on November 4 and had a huge first night on Friday, but by Sunday no one was coming to see it. In its first three days it racked up $3.8 million at nearly 1,400 theaters, but slid off afterwards.[26] Joanou had chosen to make a serious film done in black and white, with the music being treated in a similar fashion to Martin Scorcese's boxing ring in his film, *Raging Bull.* Despite the criticism, the film's dramatic intensity is undeniable. Nevertheless, it was widely panned in the United States for portraying U2 as bombastic and arrogant. A backlash was settling in, and the band was looking and sounding more defensive than they ever had before. In interviews Bono was comparing the band with the Beatles, as though U2 still needed to be justified. The criticisms hit home, and made obvious what U2 already suspected. By the end of November the film disappeared from theaters. Bono and Adam hopped into a rented Jeep Cherokee to blow off some steam, and spent three weeks driving from LA to New Orleans. Along the way they met up with *New York Times* music critic Robert Palmer, Johnny Cash, and John Prine. When they arrived in New Orleans they met Daniel Lanois, who was recording with the Neville Brothers.

In December, Roy Orbison died before the release of his *Mystery Girl* album, which contained the Bono and Edge song, "She's a Mystery to Me." A few days later "Angel of Harlem" hit number one in the United States, and at the Grammys in February U2 won Best Rock Performance for "Desire" and Best Video for "Where the Streets Have No Name." After the awards ceremony, Edge traveled to a newly liberated Moscow with David Byrne, Peter Gabriel, and Brinsley Forde from the reggae band, Aswad, to promote a Greenpeace fund-raising album. U2 had contributed "Pride (In the Name of Love)," their first release in Russia. Back in Ireland, Adam recorded two tracks with friend Sharon Shannon for her debut album. On a visit to Ireland, Nicaraguan President Daniel Ortega met with the band in a private visit.[27] U2 had been expressing support for the Sandinistas since Bono's trip to Central America, and it was appreciated.

The band was enjoying their success, if not critical acclaim, and they chose to celebrate it in their own ways. Bono and Ali had their first child, Jordan, a daughter born on Bono's birthday in May, and Edge and Aislinn had their third daughter, Blue Angel, in June. Adam suffered a personal setback when he was arrested for possession of marijuana and charged a fine of IR£25,000, to be paid to the Dublin Women's Aid Refuge. It was a lot to pay, but Paul and the rest of the band were relieved the charge was put to rest so Adam could still leave the country to tour.

Soon after, in September, U2 embarked on a four-month "Lovetown" tour of Australia, New Zealand, and Japan. They had no plans to return to the United States and expose themselves to more of the fallout from *Rattle and Hum*, a completely different strategy than U2 had previously pursued. B. B. King was supporting U2 while Aussie band Weddings Parties Anything opened the shows. The tour kicked off in Perth on September 21 and involved stretches of shows in each location, including seven in Melbourne from October 7 to October 16. When they arrived in Auckland, New Zealand, they visited Greg Carroll's family in Wanganui. In late November they flew to Japan. By this time, tour fatigue was setting in and they could feel a change was needed. The band was tired and they were ready for a new direction. As Bono said:

> If I'm honest this was the end of a journey that Bob Dylan had sent us on. In 1985, sitting backstage at his concert in Slane Castle, he said to me, "You've got to go back. You've got to understand the roots."[28]

U2 arrived in Paris for a few European shows in mid-December. While performing in Dortmund, Germany, Bono was forced to cut the show early when his voice gave out. After visiting a doctor, who advised Bono to rest his vocal chords for a week or risk permanent damage, U2 cancelled the following two shows in Amsterdam. A week later he had recovered enough for U2 to close out the 1980s with four shows at Dublin's Point Depot. In the early hours of New Year's Day 1990, U2 left the stage to go away and dream it all up again.

NOTES

1. "Amnesty Tour: Keeping the Doors Open." June 22, 1986. www .atu2.com: http://www.atu2.com/news/article.src?ID=80&Key=&Year =&Cat (accessed April 29, 2009).

2. Bill Flanagan. *U2: At the End of the World* (London: Bantam Press, 1995), 96.
3. McGee, 95.
4. *U2 by U2*, 177.
5. McGee, 98.
6. Ibid., 93.
7. *U2 by U2*, 181.
8. Ibid., 181
9. McGee, 199.
10. *U2 by U2*, 181.
11. *Rolling Stone*, 96-97.
12. *U2 by U2*, 179.
13. *Rolling Stone*, 66.
14. *U2 by U2*, 185.
15. Ibid., 186.
16. Alan, 158.
17. Assayas, 195.
18. McGee, 105.
19. Alan, 167.
20. *Rolling Stone*, 94.
21. McGee, 105.
22. Ibid., 109.
23. Ibid., 113.
24. Ibid., 118.
25. Alan, 192.
26. *Rolling Stone*, 141.
27. McGee, 125.
28. *U2 by U2*, 213.

CHAPTER SIX

Arms Around The World:
Achtung Baby & *Zooropa* (1990–1994)

Throughout 1990, U2 was looking for new directions and sharpening their ax to chop down *The Joshua Tree*. The band had reached a consensus that some form of change was necessary—they needed to stop making so much sense, stop editorializing, and get back to being artists again.

The beginning of the year found Bono and Edge working on the music for the Royal Shakespeare Company's theatrical version of *A Clockwork Orange*. Their job was to write music to take the role Beethoven's Ninth Symphony had played in the original novel. To prepare, they were listening to lots of industrial music like Front 242, Nine Inch Nails, and Einsturzende Neubauten. It was a tall order. They were exploring music that was heavier than anything they had known before to capture the novel's themes of ultra-violence and decadence. "Alex Descends into Hell for a Bottle of Milk" came from this production and later appeared as a B-side from the *Achtung Baby* sessions. However, when *A Clockwork Orange* debuted in February, Anthony Burgess wasn't impressed and dismissed the music as "neo-wallpaper."[1]

In March, Bono rented a van with his family and spent two weeks driving across the United States. During the trip he wrote a pair of songs for the Neville Brothers—"Jah Love" and "Kingdom Come."[2] When he returned to Dublin, U2 cut Cole Porter's "Night and Day" for the *Red Hot and Blue* compilation benefiting AIDS research. Recorded in Edge's basement with Moving Hearts' percussionist Noel Eccles, the song's production previewed the murky ambiguity that would surface on the next U2 album. It was a period of transitions in more ways than one. Edge and Aislinn were in the middle of a separation, and their old friend Guggi was also going through a breakup. A collective sense of unease was settling over the band, with themes of betrayal and infidelity creeping into the new songs. The band was also convinced their songwriting approach had to change. Bono had never even used the word "baby" before, but oddly found it popping up in his lyrics. The musical landscape of the late 1980s and early 1990s had shifted towards the MADchester scene based around Manchester, with bands like the Stone Roses and Happy Mondays mixing pop melodies with hip-hop beats. Hedonism was back in fashion, finding expression in raves and the drug Ecstasy. British indie band Jesus Jones had a hit with "Right Here, Right Now," with the line "watching the world wake up from history." U2 was trying to fit in and respond to this new world order.

Sometimes it's necessary to get away from family, far away, to salvage the creative process, and Bono got the idea of moving U2 to Berlin. "Domesticity is the enemy of rock 'n' roll" became one of the band's guiding mantras.[3] The Berlin Wall had fallen in November 1989 and the city was becoming a symbol of a new, resurgent Europe. In June, Paul drove there and began making arrangements at Hansa, the studio where Brian Eno had collaborated with David Bowie on his classic "Berlin Trilogy" albums. U2 arrived on October 3, 1990, the same day Germany officially reunited. Accommodation was hard to find, but through various contacts they managed to rent houses that once belonged to Soviet dignitaries. Bono ended up with former USSR president Leonid Brezhnev's villa. In the middle of the night, a family broke in and roused him out of bed in his underwear to reclaim it. Bono and the rest of the band relocated to a hotel on the east side of the city.

Hansa was a former Nazi ballroom that had been neglected and run down since Eno had last used it. Berlin in winter is cold and bleak, and despite the celebrations around reunification it failed to lift U2's spirits. When Lanois arrived to do the production, he found Larry feeling left out; he felt that the extensive use of drum machines was threatening his place in the band. Edge was increasingly focusing on dance and techno, which demanded more electronic drums, but Larry had been listening to Ginger Baker and John Bonham. He was ready to do more, but Edge was asking for less. Larry recalls:

I thought this might be the end. For the first time ever it felt like the cracks were within. And that was a much more difficult situation to negotiate.[4]

As sessions with Lanois progressed, it turned out that Edge and Bono were the only ones who truly wanted to chop down *The Joshua Tree*. The new rules were hard to adapt to, especially for Larry and Adam who were more interested in preserving the strengths of *The Joshua Tree* era. They had an ally in Lanois, but were spending too much time experimenting and playing around without finishing anything, until the day "One" emerged. Edge combined two parts he had been working on, and Bono improvised a lyric based on a note he had written to the Dalai Lama. The Tibetan spiritual leader had invited U2 to play a show called "Oneness," but it struck Bono as being a bit naïve and he sent back a note which read, "One—but not the same."[5] At this stage, Eno was playing the role of pop professor grading the hard work of his pupils. When he heard the Berlin songs he liked everything except "One." He despised it.[6] U2 went back to the drawing board and reworked the song again. They returned to Dublin in December and held a meeting. They all agreed the band was worth fighting for, and set aside their differences to finish the new album.

In January 1991, the Persian Gulf War broke out. The band was riveted to their TVs in disbelief as the United States attacked Iraq with the detached precision of a video game. It seemed absurd witnessing the conflict from the comfort of your own home, switching channels between cartoons and bloodshed with a remote control.[7] U2 was determined to express this new reality on the next album. They traveled to Tenerife, the largest of the Canary Islands, in February for video and photo shoots. Anton Corbijn photographed the band at the carnival festivities dressed up in drag, and stage designer Willie Williams flew down to discuss the next tour. Bono suggested the name "Zoo TV" after Zoo Station in Berlin, and he had dragged along a Trabant, an old East-German-made car that he wanted to use as a symbol.

By March, U2 was back in Dublin recording and things were beginning to run more smoothly. They rented a house in Dalkey called Elsinore, a mile from where Bono lived, nicknaming it "Dogtown" because it was next to a couple of kennels. Flood still had a problem with the mix for "One," and they worked on it until they captured the elusive sound everyone was happy with. Flood recalls:

There's a point in the process when the technology gets lost and you can actually use the desk as an instrument. It started to happen on that mix.[8]

The next month the band experienced a scare when their rehearsal tapes went missing and surfaced as a bootleg vinyl album called *The New U2: Rehearsals and Full Versions*. A CD version, *Salome: The Axtung Beibi Outtakes* eventually appeared the following year. A month later authorities traced the bootleg to a factory in Germany where the original tapes were found and the factory was shut down.

The band was constantly coming up with new ideas for the album and tour. Fintan Fitzgerald, U2's wardrobe man, gave Bono a pair of old 1970s sunglasses he had discovered in a warehouse from a blaxploitation film. Bono started developing an alter ego, one that would eventually evolve into the character "The Fly." It was an escape from the earnest persona he had been saddled with during the 1980s, and in some ways he was revisiting his early days in Lypton Village with friends Gavin and Guggi. Their band, the Virgin Prunes, often experimented with theater, acting out the lyrics to different songs and playing different characters. Bono said:

> The rock star I put together for myself was an identi-kit. I had Elvis Presley's leather jacket, Jim Morrison's leather pants, Lou Reed's fly shades, Jerry Lee Lewis's boots, Gene Vincent's limp. You want rock 'n' roll stuff? I'll give you some.[9]

Achtung Baby was finished by the summer of 1991. While deciding on a title, they first considered *Cruise Down Main Street*, referencing the Gulf War and the Rolling Stones' *Exile on Main Street*.[10] They settled on *Achtung Baby*, a line that came from the comedy *The Producers* that sound engineer Joe O'Herlihy often used. Bono said:

> But it's probably the heaviest record we've ever made. There is a lot of blood and guts on that record. It tells you a lot about packaging, because the press would have killed us if we'd called it anything else.[11]

The album opens with "Zoo Station," the actual name of a train station in Berlin. There was once a zoo at the location, and when it was bombed during World War II the animals were released into the streets. It was a surreal image that caught Bono's imagination. During the recording, he became frustrated with his vocals. Flood suggested distorting his voice, much like Tom Waits had been doing. [12]

Bono had become interested in the nature of authenticity in such songs as "Even Better than the Real Thing." He hit upon one of the album's guiding themes with the lyric, "we'll slide down the surface of things." He recalled:

> So with these new eyes that we had, we thought "Even Better Than the Real Thing" is actually where people live right now. People are no longer after experiences of truth. They want to know, "What is the point?" And the point is the moment. That's where we live right now, in this rave culture.[13]

"One" has become U2's signature song, popping up at weddings, parties, and even funerals for old friends. Bono has singled out the line "we *get* to carry each other" rather than "we've got to carry each other" as its defining sentiment. It suggests that the effort is a privilege, and it is not meant to be an admonishment. As the sessions were drawing to a close, Edge was inspired to add the closing guitar solo. He cut it in one take and it was mixed in 10 minutes. When it came time for the video, U2 filmed no less than three versions because they were so concerned about striking the right tone.

Bono wrote the lyric for "Until the End of the World" based on a dream he had about a conversation between Jesus and Judas after reading *The Book of Judas* by Irish poet Brendan Kennelly. When he came across the line "the best way to serve the age is to betray it," he seized on it as a way to explain the band's desire to upset expectations.[14]

About "Ultraviolet" Flood recalled:

> There was a lot of debate and a good deal of laughter, about Bono actually coming out and going "Baby." It was less to do with the political correctness of it than whether he could actually get away with singing "Baby, baby, baby, baby" and so on.[15]

Bono wrote "Love is Blindness" on piano with Nina Simone in mind, and Edge has called it one of his finest lyrics.[16] Bono kept pushing Edge for a harder, more aggressive solo, and he shreds his guitar to capture the sound.

At the end of the sessions, Edge took the final tapes and flew to LA for them to be mastered. It was one of their most difficult albums to make, and almost broke up the band. They had met the challenge of creating something new while pushing themselves to do the opposite of what they would have done before. They decided to use a collage of Anton Corbijn's photos for the cover, including a snake, a bull, an Islamic crescent moon, and a nude photo of Adam censored with a black "X."

Around this time, Island Records was sold to Polygram and the caliber of people in the organization improved. U2 had been part owner of Island and they now had a big say in how things were to be done. Paul kept a tight lid on press releases after their bad experiences with the over-hyping of *Rattle and Hum.* Throughout the summer and fall of 1991, U2 information was released exclusively through *Propaganda,* their official fan magazine. When the album hit stores in November, only Eno's provocative essay had been released to *Rolling Stone:*

> U2's records take a long time to make not because the band members are stuck for ideas but because they never stop talking about them. U2's state of mind going into this record was similar to that before *The Unforgettable Fire:* ready for something bigger, rebelling against its own stereotypes.[17]

The album was hailed as a return to form, and *Rolling Stone* awarded it 4.5 out of 5 stars. As the tour was being finalized, Bono wanted to exploit the cultural fascination with celebrity by mixing prerecorded TV programs with live feeds during the shows. Much of the spirit of Zoo TV involved U2 embracing irony and subverting expectations. For most of the 1980s, U2 saw irony as the enemy of the soul, and they revolted against people who, as Dylan put it in "All Along the Watchtower," considered "life to be but a joke." Bono was now able to slip on a mask and express himself without worrying whether what he said was true or not. He grew fond of the expression, "The mask reveals the man," paraphrasing Oscar Wilde.[18] The biggest transformation occurred when he donned the fly shades—for the first time his eyes were hidden. U2 was looking for anything that would erase the earnestness of *The Joshua Tree* era.

During their time away from the spotlight, a backlash had set in. A novelty band based in Dublin, the Joshua Trio, began performing mocking renditions of their songs. Other parodies emerged, most notoriously Negativland's 1991 crushing version of "I Still Haven't Found What I'm Looking For." Negativland remixed the song with outtakes from the program *American Top 40* that contained avuncular keener host Casey Kasem spewing expletives at his staff. As band member Mark Hosler explained:

> At one level, U2 is just these four guys making some music. But they're also not that at all. They're so huge that it becomes something else entirely. They're like Coca-Cola. As a commodity, as a corporately manufactured and distributed entertainment commodity, they—to me—become totally legitimate targets and you don't have to worry about what their feelings are or ask permission or anything.[19]

Not surprisingly, U2's label saw matters differently and sued. In October, Negativland's label, SST Records, agreed that it would stop all production of the single, recall all existing copies, and forward them to Island. SST also agreed to pay $29,292 in damages and transfer all copyright ownership of the single to Island.[20] This caused resentment among those who saw the move as blatantly hypocritical, considering that U2 would itself be guilty of the same sort of sampling/cultural appropriation during their Zoo TV tour. Although the band claimed to know nothing of the lawsuit, for the first time in U2's career they represented the worst of the corporate rock establishment.

As the tour was drawing near, U2 began assembling visual artists and video directors to create the live show, and the Trabant cars from East Germany became a dominant motif. There was a feeling of excitement and anticipation as the band knew they were exploring uncharted territory. On October 21, "The Fly" was released as the album's first single. "Mysterious Ways" and its Stephane Sednaoui video shot in Fez, Morocco, followed five weeks later. Despite the obvious change in sound and style, when *Achtung Baby* was released on November 18 it debuted at number one on Billboard, vying for the top spot with Michael Jackson's *Dangerous* and Garth Brooks's *Ropin' the Wind.*

After a few months of doing promos, the Zoo TV tour opened in Lakeland, Florida, on February 29, 1992, with the Pixies opening. Everything was bigger and more obnoxious than it had ever been before, with the band making an obvious entrance with police escorts. The U2 of old would have cringed at such a spectacle, tried to keep any extravagance a secret, and even felt ashamed, but this time they were having fun and letting it all hang out. Larry recalled:

I think a lot of people had been afraid that U2 lost its conscience, because it was dressed to be flippant and kitsch with all this rock star flamboyance. People thought we had abandoned the past. Really, we had abandoned our own insecurities. This was maybe the most political thing we'd ever done.[21]

The set design was exceptional, thanks to Willie Williams. A huge Vidiwall had been purchased that flashed all sorts of epigrams and aphorisms like "everyone's a racist except you" and "call your mother." Bono was clearly enjoying himself on stage with his TV remote and phone. He'd change channels, phone the White House, and one night in Detroit he ordered 1,000 pizzas—100 were delivered. U2 also set up a confessional box where people could confess their "sins" and have them broadcasted during encores in front of the entire audience. Zoo TV allowed the band to lighten up and revel in being rock stars for the first time. It was a theater, like an art installation, ready made for U2 to indulge in satire, irony, comedy, and great music. American writer Sam Shepard once said, "In the middle of a contradiction, that's the place to be,"[22] and Bono agreed:

I want heaven *and* hell. We've always been given this choice, to choose between the flesh and the spirit. I don't know anyone who isn't both.[23]

Zoo TV put U2 in the same live category as Pink Floyd and the Rolling Stones. It was a huge spectacle that appealed to people beyond the pop world, but it wasn't making them much money. It was costing $250,000 a day—concert or not—and the band refused to raise ticket prices, much to Paul's chagrin.[24] Bono continued to invent characters and was looking for new ways to add commentary and humor to his shtick. He came back for encores as "Mirror Ball Man," a narcissistic hypocrite in love with his own image dressed in a silver lamé suit similar to the one Elvis had worn. Folksinger Phil Ochs once put on an Elvis suit for a Carnegie Hall concert, telling the perplexed audience that the only way to save America was for "Elvis Presley to become Che Guevara."[25] Bono was a fan, and the comparison wasn't lost on him.[26]

Belly dancer Christina Petro had been added to the show for "Mysterious Ways" after one of the crew had discovered her in the parking lot before a show.[27] The tour was constantly evolving and changing, so by the end of the first leg in Vancouver on April 23 it was a different show than it had been at the start. Sometimes Edge would take the lead vocals on "Van Diemen's Land" or Larry on the traditional folk song "Dirty Old Town." Bono wasn't the only one whose image had changed; Edge took to wearing a toque and rhinestone sparkled jeans, and Adam had bleached his hair and cut it into a Mohawk.

The European leg began in Paris on May 7, and U2 found themselves rubbing shoulders with celebrities of all kinds. In Vienna, Axl Rose joined them for Dylan's "Knockin' on Heaven's Door." Rose had met the band in Los Angeles and expressed his love for "One." When they hit London, Bono met Salman Rushdie for the first time, and when they played Stockholm, U2 invited the boys of ABBA—Bjorn Ulvaeus and Benny Andersson—to help them out on a cover of their 1977 hit, "Dancing Queen."

While in Britain, the band joined Greenpeace to protest the building of a second nuclear power plant in Sellafield in northwest England. U2 dressed up in white radiation suits and recreated the Beatles' photo of *Help* on the deck of the Greenpeace ship *Solo* to highlight the issue of radioactive contamination. The plant went ahead anyway, but 15 years later Tony Blair finally agreed to shut it down. After the Greenpeace protest, they returned to Dublin for a much needed rest. Edge gave an interview with *Mondo 2000* magazine, which surreptitiously arranged for Don Joyce and Mark Hosler of Negativland to take part. When Edge found out he was surprised, but remained a good sport even when Negativland hit him up for a $20,000 loan for one of their projects. Edge said he'd think about it, asked them to put it on paper, and gave them an address to send it to.[28]

The second leg of the North American tour started August 12 at Giants Stadium; U2 was now tackling larger venues. During the acoustic set, Lou Reed joined the band on a version of "Satellite of Love" that was filmed and played on video throughout the tour. It was the height of the 1992 U.S. presidential campaign between incumbent George H. W. Bush and Arkansas governor Bill Clinton, and the band found themselves getting involved. U2 was taking to the stage every night with a video parody of Bush saying, "We will, we will rock you."

In Chicago they inadvertently booked into the same hotel Clinton was staying in. When they found out, they tried to wake him in the early morning for a party, but were steered away by secret service agents. The next morning when Clinton heard about it, he went over to Bono's suite to look for him. Bono wasn't anywhere to be found, so

Clinton waited amid the empty bottles, pizza boxes, and overflowing ashtrays as Paul searched the hotel for him. Bono had passed out in Edge's room while writing a song for Frank Sinatra—"Two Shots of Happy, One Shot of Sad." When word reached him that Governor Clinton was waiting, he bolted back to his room and the two hit it off, talking about everything from Northern Ireland to saxophones. The night they played Vancouver, Clinton won the U.S. election. Bono called the White House, leaving a message saying he wouldn't be bothering George Bush anymore—now it would be *President Clinton.*

The week after the election, while in San Diego for a show, the band drove over the border to Tijuana, Mexico, for some sightseeing and beers. As Larry was relieving himself, the police caught him and found his Swiss Army knife. Paul stepped in and offered the officers tickets to the following night's concert and all was fine.[29] U2 later flew to Mexico City for four shows and visited the ruins of Teotihuacan during their break.

Bono's personal popularity had been on the rise during the tour, and in December he became the first man in 20 years to make the cover of British *Vogue.* He was photographed with model Christy Turlington and was decked out in his leather and shades for the magazine's music issue. Around this time Adam got to know supermodel Naomi Campbell, and they soon became the focus for the paparazzi. They eventually fell in love and were engaged at the end of April. Edge was no longer with Aislinn by this time, and he was free to strike up a relationship with Morleigh Steinberg, a choreographer. She had worked with the band on the "With or Without You" video back in 1987, and had first met Edge in Los Angeles. When the original belly dancer quit the tour, Morleigh stepped in and the two were able to spend more time together.

In January 1993, U2 was invited to the Clinton inauguration, but only Larry and Adam made it. Paul and his wife, Kathy, intended to go but had to return to Ireland after his brother died suddenly of a heart attack. Adam and Larry hooked up with Michael Stipe and Mike Mills from REM, who had *Automatic for the People* out at the same time and were also big Clinton supporters. Stipe said he wanted to sing "One," and the quartet performed a stripped-down version as "Automatic Baby" for MTV. At the end of the month, Vanessa Redgrave invited Edge and Bono to a festival against racism in Hamburg, Germany. While there, they attended a performance of *The Black Rider* written by Tom Waits, William S. Burroughs, and Robert Wilson; the musical was based on an old German folktale. Bono was inspired by the play's Mephistolean-like character, Pegleg, and decided to replace Mirror Man with Mr. MacPhisto for the next leg of the tour.

Hoping it would spice up the next leg of the tour, U2 wanted to record three or four songs left over from the *Achtung Baby* sessions during their break. Bono pushed for making a full album. They only had 12 weeks, but the rest of the band took up the challenge and U2 embarked on their eighth studio album, *Zooropa*. When Johnny Cash played Dublin's Olympia Theater in February, Bono, Edge, and Larry joined the Man in Black onstage and invited him into the studio the next day to record the vocals for "The Wanderer." At the Grammys later that month, *Achtung Baby* won an award for Best Rock Vocal Performance, but lost Album of the Year to Eric Clapton's *Unplugged.*

U2 was getting some help from Eno and Flood on the new album, but time constraints were making it difficult and no one had any time for second-guessing. By May, when the European tour kicked off, they still hadn't finished. When Eno and Flood had to move on, Edge filled in as the main producer. The band was determined to follow through with what they had intended and decided to fly back to Dublin after each concert, spend a few hours in the studio and then go to bed. This went on for about a month until they finally wrapped up recording the new album.

U2 opened the Zooropa tour on May 9 in Rotterdam. A few adjustments were made for the new audiences, such as adding in clips from Leni Reifenstahl's *Triumph of the Will* and substituting flaming crosses for swastikas during "Bullet the Blue Sky." Bono was reveling in his MacPhisto persona. He had himself photographed at St. Peter's Basilica in the Vatican dressed in his gold-lamé suit and wearing red horns. For his thirty-third birthday, Gavin Friday presented him with an 8-foot cross—large enough for him to hang on it— painted blue and inscribed "Hail Bono, King of the Zoos."[30] When U2 played Berlin's Olympiastadion, the stadium Hitler built for the 1936 Olympics, for the first time, the energy level was particularly high. After the show, the police arrived to arrest soundman Joe O'Herlihy for violating sound limits, but fortunately for him he was already on a flight back to Ireland.

In June, with a new album almost set for release, U2 renewed their contract with Island Records for six albums worth $60 million, plus a $10 million advance for each album and a whopping 25 percent royalty rate on each album sold. U2 was now the highest paid act in rock history.[31] When *Zooropa* was released on July 5, 1993, it offered audiences something more abstract and looser than anything U2 had yet released. It remains a band favorite for the way it embraces technology while successfully avoiding all the usual U2 clichés, and it received positive reviews. Anthony DeCurtis from *Rolling Stone* called it "stunning" and "daring" and awarded it 4 out of 5 stars.[32] The cover includes a cartoon rendering of a lonely spaceman floating in the center of the EU flag's circle of stars; it was the second U2 album not to include a photo of the band on its cover.

The first song, "Zooropa," opens with an ad line from German carmaker Audi: "*Vorsprung durch Technik,*" translated "Advancement through Technology," along with the band's new manifesto that there was "no reason to go back." Bono said the lyric referred to his belief that "religion is the enemy of God . . . it denies the spontaneity of the spirit."[33] "Numb" compresses the information overload that Zoo TV embodied and is Edge's tour de force. He wrote the lyric after Bono's attempt fell flat. The drum loop was taken from *Triumph of the Will,*[34] and it predates the textures and stunted rhythms Radiohead would use to even greater effect a few years later on *OK Computer* with producer Nigel Godrich. Edge put together "Lemon" on a drum machine and bass using a gated guitar effect. Bono had seen a very old Super 8 film of his mother in a lemon-colored dress and was moved to explore the song's theme of cinematic voyeurism.[35]

Edge tried to build the chord progression for "Stay (Faraway, So Close!)" on the old Tin Pan Alley songs Frank Sinatra and Tony Bennett used to sing. The pop melody conceals the lyric's dark theme about a victim of physical abuse who reasons her pain away with the line, "When he hurts you, you feel alive." It was written for the Wim Wenders film of the same title. Wenders and Bono had become friends during the making of *Achtung Baby* and were admirers of each other's work. Wenders believed that U.S. culture had colonized the world's unconscious, and Bono has said the German filmmaker's film, *Paris, Texas,* was an inspiration for *The Joshua Tree.*[36]

"Dirty Day" was cobbled together from expressions Bono's father had used, including the title. It was dedicated to poet Charles Bukowski, also known as Hank, whose book of poems, *The Days run Away Like Horses Over the Hills,* was an influence on Bono. U2 had met Bukowski through Sean Penn when they played in Los Angeles.

He came to the show and Larry performed his version of "Dirty Old Town" for him.[37]

Bono wrote the lyrics to "The Wanderer" specifically for Johnny Cash. He had the Bible's Ecclesiastes, also known as "The Preacher," in mind, as well as the Dion song of the same name. There's also a little bit of Flannery O'Connor's Hazel Motes, the character from her novel *Wise Blood*, in the lyric, "I went out walking with a bible and a gun." At one point during the recording Bono thought they should rework some of the phrasing, but Cash stopped him, saying, "I like it when the rhythm's uneven. I get to do the unexpected."[38]

At the beginning of July, American filmmaker Bill Carter interviewed the band about the conflict raging in Sarajevo. Once a symbol of tolerance and infamous as the location where the assassination of Franz Ferdinand sparked World War I, Sarajevo was now descending into internecine warfare while Europe was celebrating common markets and a common currency. Bono was moved to tears while talking with Carter and agreed to play a show in the besieged city to bring attention to the war. When Paul found out, he couldn't believe it. He reminded the band of the danger of performing in the middle of a war zone, so the band decided to set up a link from Sarajevo to their concerts instead. The linkups proved to be a harsh dose of reality coming right in the middle of the shows, and were hard to deal with some nights. Larry felt they were exploiting the people's suffering, but Bono believed they were exposing it. The first linkup occurred on July 17 in Bologna, Italy, after U2 paid £100,000 to get the satellite link from the European Broadcasting Union. Via video, Carter explained that two bombs had just killed a child and injured five others within the hour. He was so close, he said, he could fly to the gig and arrive before it finished.[39] In Glasgow a few weeks later, Carter invited a woman to speak who said she would like to hear U2's music, but could only hear the screams of wounded and raped women. It cast a pall over the entire show and it never recovered. At the end of the gig, U2 agreed the next show in London would be the end of the linkups.

As a counterpoint, Bono continued to use his MacPhisto persona to comment facetiously on current events. At the next show in Wembley he said:

> Rock & roll—it's the new religion, rock & roll. I have a great interest in religion. Some of my best friends are religious leaders. The ayatollah, the pope, even the Archbishop of Canterbury—I

think he's fabulous. They're doing my work for me. . . . Nobody's going to church anymore.[40]

Salman Rushdie, author of *The Satanic Verses*, was invited on stage to speak in support of freedom of speech. Of course, MacPhisto relished the chance to ham it up with his own personal author.

U2 returned to Ireland to play a gig in Cork, where the local government tried to ban the sale of condoms at the concert. Paul reacted by personally handing them out to fans at the show.[41] The European leg wrapped up with two shows in Dublin at the end of August. During the break, Bono recorded "I Got You Under My Skin," a duet with 77-year-old Frank Sinatra. Their vocal parts were done in different cities, but they filmed a video together later in November in the back of Sinatra's limo and at his favorite bar in Palm Springs. Sinatra was beginning to suffer from memory loss, and at one point he thought he was doing a video with Sonny Bono. He apologized, and afterwards sent Bono a Cartier platinum and sapphire Pasha watch.[42]

In November, U2 flew to Australia and New Zealand for the Zoomerang and New Zooland tours, beginning in Melbourne, Australia. On tour, things were beginning to get a little wobbly. They had been on the road for two years already, and Adam was beginning to drink more than usual. The night before filming the first of two Sydney shows Adam went on a drinking binge and blacked out. The next day he was AWOL for the first Sydney gig. Larry reached him a few hours before the show, but Adam couldn't bring himself to perform. It was the first time anyone had missed a gig, and Adam's bass technician, Stuart Morgan, ended up filling in. Adam could actually hear the show going on from his hotel room, and it hit him very hard. He had let the band down; he realized that he had a serious alcohol problem and sought immediate help. The next night he was ready to play and pulled it off without a hitch, appearing unfazed for the filming of the *Zoo TV: Live from Sydney* video.

The tour wound up in Tokyo on December 10 with Big Audio Dynamite opening. Japan felt like the actual capital of Zoo TV with all its emphasis on technology. Three long years of hard work was finally coming to an end, to everyone's relief and elation.

NOTES

1. McGee, 130.

2. Ibid., 130.
3. *U2 by U2*, 216.
4. *U2 by U2*, 221.
5. Ibid., 221.
6. Stokes, 98.
7. McGee, 134.
8. Stokes, 99.
9. Assayas, 39.
10. Flanagan, 21.
11. *Rolling Stone*, 184.
12. Stokes, 96.
13. Ibid., 97.
14. *U2 by U2*, 225.
15. Stokes, 107.
16. *U2 by U2*, 228.
17. *Rolling Stone*, 167–168.
18. Flanagan, 6.
19. "Suits, Lawsuits, and Art: Negativland Takes On the Man." July 4, 1995. www.deuceofclubs.com: http://www.deuceofclubs.com/write/negativl .htm (accessed April 29, 2009).
20. McGee, 138.
21. *U2 by U2*, 237.
22. Flanagan, 80.
23. *Rolling Stone*, 188.
24. Flanagan, 83.
25. "Phil Ochs 'Carnegie Hall.'" http://home.comcast.net/~cw-trades/ ochs_carnegie_27mar70.htm (accessed April 29, 2009).
26. Flanagan, 61.
27. Ibid., 61.
28. "Negativland Interviews U2's The Edge." December 6, 2000. http:// l2g.to/negativland/: http://l2g.to/negativland/u2/the-edge-interview .html (accessed April 29, 2009).
29. McGee, 154.
30. Flanagan, 209.
31. Ibid., 218.
32. "Album Review: U2's *Zooropa*." August 3, 1993. www.rollingstone.com: http://www.rollingstone.com/reviews/album/119445/review/5942533/ zooropa (accessed April 29, 2009).
33. "Even Better Than The Surreal Thing." June 2, 1993. www.hotpress .com: http://www.hotpress.com/archive/2613082.html (accessed April 29, 2009).
34. Stokes, 114.
35. *U2 by U2*, 248–249.
36. Stokes, 117.
37. Ibid., 121.

38. *U2 by U2*, 249.
39. McGee, 164.
40. *Rolling Stone*, 210.
41. McGee, 166.
42. *U2 by U2*, 255.

Bono Vox, the lead singer of the Irish rock group U2, performs on stage at Madison Square Garden in New York City, April 1, 1985. (AP Photo/Ron Frehm)

George Michael of Wham, center-left, concert promoter Harvey Goldsmith, U2 lead singer Bono Vox, Paul McCartney, and Queen lead singer Freddie Mercury perform during the Live Aid famine relief concert finale on July 13, 1985 at Wembley Stadium in London, England. (AP Photo/Joe Schaber)

Bono and The Edge (left) opened their world tour, April 2, 1987, before a soldout crowd at the Activity Center on the campus of Arizona State University in Tempe. U2 kicked off a 14-city tour of the United States, promoting their new album The Joshua Tree. *(AP Photo/Tom Story)*

Lead singer Bono spray paints "Rock 'n Roll" on a concrete fountain sculpture in San Francisco on November 11, 1987, during a surprise 45-minute concert that drew an estimated 20,000 people. (AP Photo/Ken Howard)

Members of U2 pose on November 22, 1989, for photographers prior to a press conference held at the Irish Ambassador's residence in Tokyo. The group was on a concert tour through Japan. They are, from left: Larry, Bono, Adam, and Edge. (AP Photo/Sadayuki Mikami).

The Edge, Larry Mullen, Bono, and Adam Clayton, left to right, members of U2, pose for photographers during a New York news conference on February 12, 1997, announcing their PopMart Tour '97. The conference was held at a Kmart department store near New York's Greenwich Village. (AP Photo/Richard Drew)

Members of U2 pose for a studio portrait in April 1997. From left: guitarist Edge, drummer Larry Mullen, lead vocalist Bono and bass player Adam Clayton. The four kicked off their international PopMart tour on April 25, 1997, at Sam Boyd Stadium in Las Vegas. (AP Photo/HO/Anton Corbijn)

Bono performs with U2 during "We Are One: Opening Inaugural Celebration at the Lincoln Memorial" in Washington, D.C., on January 18, 2009. (AP Photo/Alex Brandon)

CHAPTER SEVEN

Too Much Is Not Enough: *Pop* & PopMart (1994–1998)

When U2 returned home from their three-year journey, they had a very hard time adjusting to normal family life. The frenetic pace of the Zoo TV tour left the band restless about their future. How could they top it? What could they do next? Would they ever tour again?

In January 1994 Bono inducted one of his heroes, Bob Marley, into the Rock and Roll Hall of Fame, saying, "He raced to the edges, embracing all extremes, creating a oneness. His oneness."[1] The next week he attended the Golden Globe awards where U2 was competing against themselves in the Best Original Song category for "Stay (Far Away, So Close!)" and "You Made Me the Thief of Your Heart" from the film *In the Name of the Father*. Both songs lost to Bruce Springsteen's "Streets of Philadelphia." Later, at the Grammys in New York, Bono presented Frank Sinatra with the Living Legend Award, calling him the "big bang of pop" in a speech that has since become one of his most memorable.

Adam and Larry were both looking for projects outside of the band to re-energize their performance skills. They relocated to New York, took music lessons, and played on Nanci Griffith's album *Flyer*. They also recorded "The Theme to Mission Impossible," which made the U.S. top 10 in June the following year. Back in Europe, Bono came up with the idea of U2 purchasing a single house in the south of France as a retreat to relax and create in, but he and Edge were the only ones who bought in. They purchased a property with two houses in the village of Eze, just outside of Nice on the Côte d'Azur, where the two spent most of their time in the summer of 1994. Bono struck up a friendship with Michael Hutchence, the lead singer from INXS, and hosted frequent parties along the beachfront with new and old friends who had come from Ireland to join the festivities. The summer spiraled into a whole year as a new love affair began for music in general. Britpop was in full bloom, and Edge and Bono were indulging in it as pure fans.

In the past there had been some tension between Brian Eno and U2 over songwriting attribution because Eno felt he should have received credit for some of his contributions. Everyone agreed they made great music together, so they decided to collaborate formally on a new project under a different name. They initially thought they would work on the soundtrack for Peter Greenaway's film, *The Pillow Book,* but that fell through. Eno then came up with another idea for an album in which each song would represent a soundtrack for a different fictional film. The project became known as *Original Soundtracks 1* by Passengers. U2 spent two weeks in London's Westside studios with Eno. He prepared the studio with rugs and prints from India, Africa, and the Arab world. The sessions were very free-form, and some heated exchanges occurred when Eno felt the band was not taking it as seriously as he'd like. Feelings in the band were mixed— most enjoyed the music, but Larry didn't particularly like it, saying, "There's a thin line between interesting music and self-indulgence. We crossed it on the Passengers record."[2]

Nevertheless, the songs are extraordinary, completely different from anything they'd ever done before, and, as is typical for Eno, years ahead of their time. The album included a Japanese track, "Ito Okashi," whereas "A Different Kind of Blue" or "Elvis Ate America" would not be out of place on *Zooropa.* One of the most enduring, "Miss Sarajevo," was an attempt to write a libretto for the great opera tenor Luciano Pavarotti. The song arose from an actual event; a group of women from Sarajevo had organized a beauty contest with sashes that read, "Do they really want to kill us?" Bill Carter eventually turned it into a film, and Bono has since called it his favorite U2 song.[3]

In January 1995, U2's official magazine, *Propaganda,* issued a fanclub-only CD called *Melon. Melon* contained nine remixed songs including "Lemon," "Numb," Mysterious Ways," and "Stay." It was very well received and furthered U2's explorations into techno and dance. The next month, Bono and Edge left the gadgets behind to collaborate with veteran folksinger Christy Moore on a song called "North and South of the River" about the tensions between Northern Ireland and the Republic. Bono was also working on a version of Leonard Cohen's "Hallelujah" for the *Tower of Song* compilation. When he finished, he asked DJ Howie B., whom Adam and Larry had worked with on the soundtrack to *Mission Impossible*, to remix it. When they heard it, the rest of the band was impressed and filed away his name for future reference. It's an unconventional cover that abandons the original song's melody for a spoken-word rendition and features jazz trumpet. At the end of the month, Bono fulfilled a dream by joining Prince at the Pod in Dublin on "The Cross," his gospel-ballad from *Sing O' the Times.*

To cut "Hold Me, Thrill Me, Kiss Me" for the *Batman Returns* soundtrack, U2 enlisted Nellee Hooper, who had worked with Bjork and Massive Attack. The film producers had offered Bono $5 million to play his MacPhisto character alongside Jim Carrey's Riddler, but he declined.[4] On June 14, Rory Gallagher, one of Edge's original inspirations, died from complications linked to a liver transplant. Edge paid tribute, calling him "a very sensitive man and a great musician."[5] Gallagher had been one of the most successful international stars Ireland had ever produced before U2 came along.

During this time, Pavarotti had been nagging Bono and the band to come to his hometown of Modena, Italy, and play at his upcoming charity. In July, he dropped in at U2's Dublin studios and Bono finally relented, agreeing to attend with Edge and Eno to perform "Miss Sarajevo." They premiered it at the annual Pavarotti and Friends concert on September 12, along with an orchestral version of "One." Bono and Edge brought their families, and at one point Pavarotti sang "Happy Birthday" for Eno's wife while Edge's father sang along. Princess Diana was in attendance and met everyone, and Bono's father, who had been a bit of a Republican, was charmed after shaking her hand.

Larry and Ann, his long time girlfriend, had their first son, Aaron Elvis, in October. He was having some back problems and had to have surgery for an old drumming injury. The band was eager to start working with Howie B., their choice for their next producer, and they went into the studio before Larry was ready. It grated him a bit, but he understood their enthusiasm to begin working. For the next album the band agreed they wanted to fuse the sweet pop of a band like the Spice Girls with rhythm loops, sequencing, and gritty industrial sounds.

In November, Passengers' *Original Soundtracks I* was released. *Rolling Stone* wrote that it lacked inspiration and gave it a meager 2 out of 5 stars.[6] Edge and Bono's contribution to the James Bond film *Goldeneye* also appeared, with Tina Turner on vocals. In December, Dubliner Ronny Drew's *Dirty Rotten Shame* was released with a track co-written with Bono called, "Drinkin' in the Day." Bono had expressed his admiration for the band back in 1987 when they had participated in a Dubliners' tribute on RTÉ. For the New Year festivities, Bono and Ali flew to Sarajevo to celebrate the newly declared truce.

Eno had had enough of U2 for the time being and wasn't interested in the new album, but Flood, their trusty engineer, still was. It would become the first album since 1984's *The Unforgettable Fire* that wouldn't feature Eno's contribution. Nellee Hooper, who had worked on "Hold Me, Thrill Me, Kiss Me," was also onboard, and producer Steve Osborne filled in for Steve Lillywhite. The recording took place in U2's new studio in Dublin, overlooking the picturesque Grand Canal. The band was focused on combining pop and club culture without resorting directly to electronica, as they had on *Zooropa*. As Adam said, "You have to keep in touch with what's going on at the cutting edge of youth culture and of contemporary music."[7] *Pop*, as the album would be called, was the sound of U2 trying to catch up with the Prodigy and Massive Atttack. Bono said:

> One of my definitions of art is the discovery of beauty in unexpected places. This was really the theme of *Pop*: big subjects for the basement.[8]

Edge was getting sick and tired of Britpop, dismissing it as boring and lacking innovation, but he made an exception for Oasis, saying that their songs were strong enough to transcend any genre. The rest of the band was ready for another experimental album like *Achtung Baby*, one that could tackle big cultural themes, but also get on the radio. In the middle of the sessions, Paul booked U2's next tour, and suddenly deadlines were looming. Larry went back to the studio in February—a bit earlier than he should have—and scrambled to get his drum parts down.

Pop opens with the swirling gyrations of "Discothèque," a track Howie B. had a very hard time nailing down: "It was outrageous. It had gotten to the stage where I couldn't speak, I was that ill."[9] The band was making a statement, and it was crucial they get it right. They had been out of the public eye for a while and felt they needed a brash, bold song to get everyone's attention. The title alone signaled U2 had crossed into a forbidden zone where platform shoes and gold medallions reigned. On "Mofo," U2 embraces gritty dance music without any inhibitions. Bono speaks directly to his deceased mother, asking, "Mother, am I still your son?" He called it "the most exposed moment in the hardest tune on the record. It was as if my life was in that song."[10] Old friend Gavin Friday, who is listed in the album's liner notes as "Consultant Poptician," concurred:

> There's no question about it, "Mofo" is one of my favourite tracks. To me it sounds like Led Zeppelin after taking an E.[11]

"Last Night on Earth" has more of a conventional rock groove, and they were working on it right until the last minute before the album was sent to New York to be mastered. Bono recalled:

> The chorus only came into my head at about 4 o'clock in the morning on the final night. My voice was completely shot, which is why we put so much echo on it and Edge sang along with me to cover it up.[12]

After working on the album for months, they needed a break. In May, U2 flew to Miami, Florida, and ended up smoking a lot of cigars and checking out what the city had to offer. Everything U2 experienced was put into the song "Miami," from the "surgery in the air" to the two new suits Bono had bought—one pink, the other blue. While there, Bill Graham, a friend and mentor from *Hot Press*, died, and U2 immediately returned to Dublin. Edge and Bono were pallbearers at the funeral and performed Leonard Cohen's "Tower Of Song" as a tribute.

After reassembling in the studio the band cut "The Playboy Mansion," an attempt at sleazy lounge music, with Bono asking if he has what it takes to get through the gates of the mansion, a metaphor for paradise of luxurious trash. "Wake Up Dead Man" was a leftover from *Zooropa;* the title came from an old chain gang song from the

U.S. South. Edge wrote the first verse and chorus as an appeal to Jesus to wake up and save his soul. It's a true howl of despair that finishes in the gutter an album that began as high as the stars.

The cover art included close-up headshots of all four members glossed over with an alloy sheen of rainbow colors. With *Pop*, U2 had initially wanted to make a party album, but the dawn crept in to shine a cold light on the leftovers. The title was a deliberate attempt to mislead—pop music is usually anathema to a rock audience, and U2 was trying to challenge expectations. Bono said, "I thought 'pop' was a term of abuse, it seemed sort of insulting and lightweight."[13] He felt the tone of the album was the opposite of pop and that it resembled a conversation with God—it should have actually been called "U2, Lighten Up."[14]

The new tour, PopMart, had already been booked, and the band had no choice but to finish the recording even though they knew the album needed a bit more work. It was feeling unfocused and lacked a central theme, mainly because too many producers were involved and the technology was getting the best of the process. Throughout the recording Bono felt like he was losing his voice, and there is an uncertainty to his singing, as though he was holding back for fear he might rip his vocal chords to shreds.

Pop was greeted with mixed reviews when it appeared on March 3. *Rolling Stone* wrote it was "some of the greatest music of their lives,"[15] while the BBC noted U2 was "straining to keep up with the Zeitgeist."[16] Nevertheless, it roared up to number one in 27 countries the week it was released, but quickly dropped off. It was replaced only a week later in the UK by the Spice Girls' *Spice*. After *Pop* was finished, Bono got into a peculiar controversy with the Irish National Parents Council when he was asked to donate his favorite childhood toy for a Romanian orphan fund-raiser. He donated a sketch of his penis titled, "Me Rattler."[17]

"Discothèque" was chosen as *Pop*'s first single, and for the video the band dressed up as the Village People dancing inside a giant mirror ball. At one point Bono actually humps the camera with his crotch. The single and video were released in January 1997, before the album, but the United States was a very different place than they expected. The remnants of grunge still lingered in the watered-down form of the Smashing Pumpkins and the Goo Goo Dolls, and the dance culture U2 had been enjoying in Europe was still an underground phenomenon.

U2 decided to launch the PopMart tour by holding a press conference at a K-Mart, a cheap, discount department store in New York City, as far away from glamour as anyone could get. The band appeared in the lingerie department singing "Holy Joe," the B-side of "Discothèque." Bono thought U2 was following in the footsteps of pop artists like Roy Lichtenstein and Andy Warhol, but the band soon realized their music betrayed any attempt to come off as flippant or shallow, and the joke eventually turned on them. They seemed unsure as to their intentions—were they making a mockery of pop culture or celebrating it? *Pop* did neither, and in the final analysis, the band lacked the panache and conviction to pull off their grandiose plans.

The PopMart tour took an enormous amount of money to run—over $200,000 a day. U2 stage designer Willie Williams incorporated images from consumer culture, such as the golden arches of McDonalds, into the visual behemoth. U2 wanted to outdo Zoo TV and invested in ridiculous stage props like a huge 40-foot lemon and a 100-foot cocktail stick topped with a giant olive. They had risked bankruptcy with Zoo TV, and this time Paul found an outside promoter from Toronto, Michael Cohl, to sponsor the tour for a reported US$100 million. To promote the tour U2 joined ABC television and filmed an hour-long documentary called *U2: A Year in Pop*, with Dennis Hopper narrating. Bono admitted he had one of the worst haircuts of the 1980s, spawning the "Irish mullet" in a failed attempt to copy David Bowie on the cover of *Aladdin Sane*. Ratings for the program were abysmal, the worst-ever at the time for a nonpolitical show. To make matters worse, they released their next single, "Staring at the Sun," in the middle of April, convinced they had a number one hit. They ended up producing a bland video with fluorescent-lit closeups of the band that was widely panned as dull and incoherent. When the single only reached number 26 on Billboard, they soon realized they'd have to start working a lot harder because tickets for the upcoming tour weren't selling out either.

PopMart's opening show in Las Vegas on April 25 didn't go over well and suffered from technical problems. It was taking them more time than they thought to work out the bugs and adjust to the new material in a live setting. After openers Rage Against the Machine finished, Bono mounted the stage dressed in plastic bubble pants draped with a boxer's cape that was emblazoned on the back with PopMart's golden arch. Edge was dressed in a cowboy hat with a handlebar moustache, Adam wore an orange jumpsuit with a chemical mask, and Larry dressed as he always did, in a T-shirt and trousers. Within a few weeks, some in the press began writing the tour off as "FlopMart."[18]

The next video, "Last Night on Earth" was shot in Kansas City, with beat author William S. Burroughs making a cameo. Before the single was released in July, the band went into the studio to re-record it in an effort to address the shortcomings of the original. In June, U2 participated in the Tibetan Freedom Concert along with Patti Smith, the Beastie Boys, and Sonic Youth. U2 performed a five-song set including "Gone," "Mysterious Ways," "One," "Until the End of the World," and "Please." Only "One" made it onto the album release of the concert, which also featured a short two-minute interview with Bono.

At the end of the month Oasis supported U2 in Oakland, and after the show they went out on the town. At 4 a.m. they were at the Tosca Café, a famed hangout in San Francisco's North Beach neighborhood, blasting "O Sole Mio" on the jukebox.[19] U2 outlasted Noel and Liam Gallagher, who returned to their hotel to sleep while Bono and company stayed up to watch the sunrise over the Golden Gate Bridge. During their sets, U2 began adding oddball covers like Neil Diamond's "Sweet Caroline" and Elvis' "Suspicious Minds." In Los Angeles, Davy Jones from the Monkees even joined the band for "Daydream Believer." The U.S. leg of PopMart finally wrapped up in Foxboro, Massachusetts, on July 2.

The European tour opened a few weeks later in Rotterdam, where U2 began pulling in larger crowds. In Oslo, their huge lemon broke down during the encore and the band had to exit out the back, down a ladder, in order to return to the stage. It was a little frightening and embarrassing at the time, but the story has since entered U2 folklore as one of the band's more hilarious experiences. For Edge's birthday in August the band rented a yacht off the coast of Finland, and the next night in Helsinki, Morleigh, who was noticeably pregnant, joined them onstage to belly dance during "Mysterious Ways." Around this time, Larry and Bono appeared on a tribute album for the "singing brakeman," Jimmie Rodgers, playing "Dreaming With Tears in My Eyes." Despite their forays into dance culture, the band remained loyal to American roots music.

The crowd was noticeably subdued when the band played Dublin on August 31, the day after Princess Diana's death. During "MLK" a Warholian image of Diana appeared on the screen in tribute. Her death came as a complete shock to the band. They had met her in 1995 at Pavarotti's charity concert and had been taken by her charm. In the wake of this upset U2 kept to their word and returned to play Sarajevo the next month. They were welcomed like heroes and provided the population with a semblance of normality after the recent brutal conflict. Muslims, Croats and Serbs from all over the divided region, many of whom had been bitter enemies only a year before, gathered to hear U2's message of pop and peace. There were NATO peacekeepers everywhere, and on either side of the old, battered Kosovo Stadium were graveyards.

Unfortunately, Bono had lost some of his voice by the night of the concert, but the audience helped him out, and Brian Eno made the trip to sing "Miss Sarajevo." U2 then went on to play their first concerts in Greece and Israel.

U2 started the third leg of PopMart in Toronto on October 26. Howie B. was kicked off the tour when he was caught with a small amount of marijuana crossing the border from Canada into the United States. More difficulties awaited when they returned to the United States. One of the lowest points came at a Tampa Bay show in November, where they played to only 20,000 fans in a stadium that held 75,000. Soon after, news came that Michael Hutchence had committed suicide. He had gotten involved with Bob Geldof's ex-wife, Paula Yates, and he and Bono had lost touch. It was a messy divorce, but she and Hutchence fell deeply in love. He was found dead at Sydney's Ritz-Carlton Hotel. The coroner ruled suicide, but Yates never accepted the verdict and died of a heroin overdose in 2000. At U2's next show, "Gone" was dedicated to him.

When they played Mexico at the beginning of December, they ran into trouble with President Ernesto Zedillo's two sons. They crashed the concert, and their bodyguards seriously injured Jerry Meltzer and Jerry Mele, the head of U2 security. The next day the band went to meet the President and they exchanged harsh words. Zedillo believed his sons' version of events and refused to issue a public apology. Mele later sued the Mexican government and the concert promoter and won a substantial settlement in 1999. U2 left Mexico to play Vancouver, and finished the North American tour on December 12 in Seattle.

After a break for the holidays, U2 took PopMart south to play for the first time in Brazil, Argentina, and Chile. They opened on January 27 in Rio de Janeiro. While in Buenos Aires, U2 brought a large group of the Mothers de Plaza de Mayo onstage to perform "One," and the shows ended with "Mothers of the Disappeared" as the women recited the names of their missing loved ones. In Santiago, Chile, Bono dedicated a song to Victor Jara and U2 invited some of the women onstage who had lost family during the reign of General Pinochet's junta. Bono made an emotional plea to Pinochet to "give the dead back to the living."[20] Like the country, the audience was divided between supporters and opponents of Pinochet, and the air was filled with cheers and boos.

In February U2 left for the Australian leg of the tour, and made a surprise stop in Johannesburg, South Africa, to visit the ESP nightclub before arriving in Perth to play their first show. At a press conference at the Burswood Dome, Bono said:

> The job of rock'n'roll, if it has any kind of job at all, is to blow people's heads. It's a hard call to turn a shopping mall or a supermarket into a cathedral but that's actually what we're trying to do. We're trying to find the spirit in the machine, if you like.[21]

At the end of their performances in Australia they paid tribute to Michael Hutchence with "One." His image flickered across the video screen as the band segued into the defiant, "Wake Up Dead Man" before leaving the stage to the strains of the INXS's ballad, "Never Tear Us Apart." It left many in the crowd in tears, and turned Pop-Mart into a cathedral as Bono had wished. He later said about the Hutchence tribute; "This is his country. This is his house and we can't help thinking about him when we're here."[22]

U2 went on to Tokyo and Osaka in Japan, and finally wound up in South Africa again. They met Archbishop Desmond Tutu and toured Robben Island in Cape Town where Nelson Mandela had been imprisoned for two decades. At the end of April, U2 had a cameo in the 200th episode of *The Simpsons* called "Trash of the Titans." When PopMart hit Springfield, U2 joined Homer for the song, "The Garbage Man Can" to the tune of "The Candy Man." It was a hilarious self-parody that spoofed the band as wankers with overbites and Adam as a passionate collector of spoons. Later in the year it won an Emmy Award for Outstanding Animated Program.

After returning to Dublin, U2 found out they had made the *Guinness Book of World Records* for playing to 3.9 million people, the largest ever audience at the time. *Pop* had sold 7 million copies, not too bad for U2's self-confessed low point.

NOTES

1. McGee, 172.
2. "U2 Quotes by Larry Mullen." www.threechordsandthetruth.net: http://www.threechordsandthetruth.net/u2quotes/larry.htm (accessed April 29, 2009).
3. "Just the 2 of U." February 27, 2009. www.irishtimes.com: http://www.irish times.com/newspaper/theticket/2009/0227/1224241848766.html (accessed April 29, 2009).
4. McGee, 179.
5. Ibid., 179.
6. "Album Review: Passengers: *Original Soundtracks 1.*" December 14, 1995. www.rollingstone.com: http://www.rollingstone.com/artists/passengers/albums/album/311260/review/5943352/original_soundtracks_1 (acessed April 29, 2009).
7. "The History of Pop." March 19, 1997. www.hotpress.com: http://www.hotpress.com/archive/392675.html (accessed April 29, 2009).
8. *U2 by U2*, 266.
9. Stokes, 125.
10. Ibid., 129.
11. Ibid., 128.
12. Ibid., 132.
13. "Pop." www.u2.com: http://www.u2.com/discography/index/album/albumId/4011/tagName/studio_albums (accessed April 29, 2009).
14. *U2 by U2*, 269.
15. Album Review: U2's "*Pop.*" March 20, 1997. www.rollingstone.com: http://www.rollingstone.com/artists/u2/albums/album/321527/review/5942462/popI (accessed April 29, 2009).
16. "Straining to keep up with the zeitgeist." February 13, 2009. www.bbc.co.uk: http://www.bbc.co.uk/music/reviews/dvn8 (accessed April 29, 2009).
17. McGee, 184.
18. "Pop Not Flop." August 6, 1997. www.hotpress.com: http://www.hotpress.com/archive/415904.html (accessed April 29, 2009).
19. McGee, 194.
20. Ibid., 203.
21. "U2 Spirit in the Cathedral," Michael Dwyer. February 17, 1998. http://www.u2tours.com/displaymedia.src?ID=19980217&XID=659&Return (accessed April 29, 2009).
22. Ibid.

CHAPTER EIGHT

A Sort of Homecoming: *All That You Can't Leave Behind* (1998–2002)

When U2 returned to Dublin, the Northern Ireland peace process was trying to gain traction. The vote on the Good Friday Agreement was going to be close. U2 had always felt they embodied the type of tolerance and diversity Ireland could represent. Edge and Adam were born in England, Bono had Protestant and Catholic parents, and Larry was Catholic. When they were asked to perform in support of the YES campaign, they agreed, but stipulated one condition: that Ulster Unionist leader David Trimble and Social Democratic and Labour Party leader John Hume appear together on stage.

The concert took place at Belfast's Waterfront Hall in May, with Bono and Edge performing with the Northern Ireland band, Ash, on the Beatles' "Don't Let Me Down" and then with Larry and Adam on "One." Bono took the opportunity to recreate the famous Bob Marley photo with Jamaican politicians Michael Manley and Edward Seaga at the One Love Peace Concert in 1978. He stood in the middle of Hume and Trimble, took their hands and raised them to the sky, asking the audience for a minute's silence for all those who had died in Ireland's sectarian conflict. In the end, the YES vote won by only a few points. Bono has since called his participation the greatest honor of his life.[1]

Then, in August, horror struck when a bomb went off in Omagh, Northern Ireland, killing 29 people and injuring 220. It had a profound effect on the entire island, and Bono wrote the lyrics to "Peace on Earth" to articulate his sorrow. His father, Bob, had come down with cancer, and Bono's voice still hadn't improved. Later in the fall, and without telling Ali or the band, he underwent surgery to discover if he had any sign of cancer in his throat. It turned out negative, but he felt it was a major brush with mortality. Ali was also pregnant again. Through all these life-and-death occurrences, Bono decided U2 should make an emotionally raw album, celebrate life's essentials, and cut out any technique in favor of the songs.

In September, U2 shot the video for "The Sweetest Thing" on the streets of Dublin with director Kevin Godley. It's a humorous portrait of Bono offering Ali gifts as a way of saying sorry for missing her birthday. The song had originally been released in 1987 as a B-side on the "Where the Streets Have No Name" single. It also appeared on the soundtrack to the 1988 film *Scrooged* covered by the New Voices of Freedom, the same gospel choir that appeared in *Rattle and Hum*. U2 had always liked the song, and their re-recorded version later topped the charts in Ireland and Canada.

When John Hume and David Trimble won the Nobel Peace Prize in October, Bono hosted a dinner party at his home. Later in the month he joined Edge and Adam to kick off Amnesty International's Irish campaign. He addressed the crowd on O'Connell Street in central Dublin:

> One of the biggest problems in the world is the cynical idea that the world can't be changed and that politics and economics are too complicated to deal with. But with Amnesty it's simple; you can write a postcard and make a difference to the life of someone who is in jail or suffering human rights abuses.[2]

Marianne Faithfull's *A Perfect Stranger* album was also released this month, which included "Conversation On A Barstool," written by Edge and Bono back in 1989.

The band was also putting the final touches on *The Best of U2: 1980–1990*, giving them some space to work on a new album. It debuted at number two in the United States behind Alanis Morissette's *Supposed Former Infatuation Junkie*, and had the highest first-week sales of any greatest hits album. U2 also launched Kitchen Records, a new dance label named after their nightclub in the basement of the Clarence Hotel. They then played RTÉ's *The Late Show* and dedicated their performance to the victims of the Omagh bombing. They performed "All I Want Is You" and "North and South of the River," their song written with Christy Moore.

After their experience working with the politburo of producers on *Pop,* U2 was keen to return with Brian Eno and Daniel Lanois for their next album. Eno immediately pressed the band to get into the studio and quickly record what they could. He thought that once they had some songs down, they could pick and choose what they wanted. The band went into their Hanover Quay studio and jammed around for about three months to loosen up and develop ideas. Larry wanted to return to basics and go back to working with just four guys in a room. This time no deadlines were set, and U2 promised themselves they would finish 11 songs before thinking about anything else. They recorded like they did in the early days—all in one room together. During the sessions, Edge came up with "Kite" and Bono finally found his voice on the lyric, blowing everyone away with its power. It turned out that he had had some allergies that were affecting his voice. He got them treated, but one side effect of the medication turned his eyes red, so he began wearing sunglasses.

Apart from working on new material, Bono was also getting involved in other activities that would eventually raise tensions with the other members. In February, a film crew began shooting Bono's film, *The Million Dollar Hotel,* with old friend Wim Wenders directing. Later in the month, Bono wrote an editorial for the *Guardian* newspaper to help launch the Jubilee 2000 campaign, and he threw himself into the effort to reduce Third World debt. For him the issue wasn't about charity, but about justice. Bono frequently said he came from a long line of traveling salesmen on his mother's side, and he put this hereditary skill to work by beginning to lobby world leaders to forgive the debt. In the beginning, his great benefactor in the United States was Eunice Shriver, John F. Kennedy's older sister. She introduced Bono to her son, Bobby Shriver, who supported the cause and helped get it into motion. The movement grew, and involved meetings with everyone from Bill Clinton and Tony Blair to World Bank President Jim Wolfensohn and Pope John Paul II. His efforts were producing results, but his responsibilities in U2 were being strained. The band supported his causes, but when they were set up and ready to record, it was frustrating to have to wait around for their vocalist to arrive.

At the Grammys that year Bono sang on Kirk Franklin's "Lean on Me" with Mary J. Blige in what *Rolling Stone* called the awards' "Most Out-of-Place Performance."[3] A week later he popped up in Las Vegas with Bob Dylan singing "Knockin' on Heaven's Door," and then inducted Bruce Springsteen into the Rock and Roll Hall of Fame, his third after the Who in 1990 and Bob Marley in 1994. Of Springsteen, he said:

> They call him the Boss. Well that's a bunch of crap. He's not the boss. He works FOR us. More than a boss, he's the owner, because more than anyone else, Bruce Springsteen owns America's heart.[4]

In June, Bono was at the G8 Summit in Cologne, Germany, to present a petition signed by 17 million people supporting debt relief. With Ali and Edge he took part in a human chain around the G8 facility and met with Tony Blair. Bono then joined Bob Geldof, economist Jeffrey Sachs, and other supporters of Jubilee 2000 to visit Pope John Paul II in Italy. The pope gave a speech in support of debt relief, and Bono gave the pontiff a book of Seamus Heaney's poetry and handed him his sunglasses. The pope put them on, and Bono dubbed him the world's "first funky pontiff."[5]

Around this time Bono recorded a new song, "New Day," and recorded a video with Wyclef Jean for NetAid, an antipoverty organization. Although it conveyed the best of intentions, it fell woefully short as a pop song and seemed more like a *Sesame Street* jingle. Later in the fall, Bono helped launch NetAid at Giants Stadium in New Jersey, Wembley in London, and the Palais des Nations in Geneva. Despite a lineup that included George Michael, David Bowie, Puff Daddy, Wyclef Jean, and Mary J. Blige, the event was poorly attended and generated little interest. People wondered if "donor's fatigue" had finally set in, or if Bono had lost his juju.

Bono's peripatetic schedule was clashing with Eno's usual work ethic, which required 100 percent focus to maximize potential in the studio. But it didn't seem to be hampering his input into the music. He was constantly writing lyrics and delivering solid performances when it mattered most. Bono usually worked in creative spurts, as with the vocal for "In a Little While," which he nailed in a few takes. Still, the songs for the new album were taking longer than Eno or the rest of the band would have liked.

U2 took two months off in November to work on the soundtrack for Bono's film, *The Million Dollar Hotel.* During the making of *Rattle and Hum,* he was at the actual Million Dollar Hotel in Los Angeles and was inspired to collaborate on the script with screenwriter

Nicholas Klein. It made a lasting impression, and more than 10 years later he asked his friend Wim Wenders to direct and Mel Gibson and Milla Jovovich to star. They shot it in only 34 days, and it eventually won a Silver Bear at the Berlin Film Festival, but it was panned by most critics. Gibson later tried to distance himself from the project, calling it "as boring as a dog's arse," although he later apologized.[6]

Hal Wilner produced the soundtrack with musicians Brad Mehldau, Bill Frisell, and John Hassell. Bono talked Daniel Lanois into collaborating on it, but one of the strongest songs, "The Ground Beneath Her Feet," was co-written with Salman Rushdie. In the years after Iran's Ayatollah Khomeini ordered a fatwa against Rushdie for writing *The Satanic Verses,* he turned up at Bono's place in Dublin for some rest and relaxation. While there, he wrote the lyrics and presented them to Bono who came up with some music. Both he and Lanois thought it might be good enough for U2, but no one showed any interest. U2 refers to ballads as "salads," and they thought this one needed some more spice so they passed.[7] Lanois added some pedal steel to the song's languorous rhythm, and in January they shot a video with Wenders directing and Rushdie making an appearance. When Island saw it, they held it back because they didn't like the film and were afraid too much promotion would ultimately reflect badly on U2's upcoming release.[8]

The other songs on the album are mood pieces, mellow and understated. "Never Let Me Go" is a smooth crooner with acoustic bass ebbing up against the silent spaces in the mix. "Stateless" recalls a slowed-down leftover from *Zooropa,* and "Falling At Your Feet" is a graceful pop song with Lanois' trademark falsetto meshing seamlessly with Bono's lower register. The album was released in March with three U2 tracks—"The Ground Beneath Her Feet," "Stateless," and "The First Time"—and received generally positive reviews.

U2 was awarded the Freedom of Dublin City in March 2000 and performed a four-song set, including the first live performance of "The Sweetest Thing." One of the privileges of being a "freeman" is the right to graze sheep on public land. The next day, Bono and Edge went out to Stephen's Green with two sheep and let them run wild. During the same ceremony, Burmese Democracy advocate and 1991 Nobel Laureate Aung San Suu Kyi was honored. The band wasn't familiar with her, but they did some research and later wrote "Walk On" as a tribute. When Bono turned 40 in May, Ali hired a vintage plane to fly them around Europe with a handful of his friends. At the end of the month, he finally met Nelson Mandela for the first time at the Laureus Sports Awards in Monaco.

By the end of the 1990s, U2 was a brand in decline. Their albums weren't selling, and neither were their live shows. From *Zooropa* through *Pop, Passengers,* and *Million Dollar Hotel,* U2 was sounding like a band trying to mask its soul, stepping back from the passion that made them so vital and popular. By enlisting the duo of Eno and Lanois they began creating a soul-filled album without backing away from the technology that had become their trademark. Larry recalled:

> People thought *All That You Can't Leave Behind* was a return to the U2 of old. Technology is a big part of what we do. I think on this album we were a little more subtle with it.[9]

Edge was using his old Gibson Explorer guitar from the early days when he came up with the riff for "Beautiful Day." Bono didn't want to use it at first because it sounded like a step backwards. In the end they decided to keep it, and Eno and Lanois added some strings before Bono did his vocals. Lanois recalled:

> I had this image of Bono, singing about beauty in the midst of flying pieces of metal and mayhem.[10]

Producer and old friend Jimmy Iovine dropped by Dublin and listened to the track in progress. There was no doubt in his mind that they were onto a monster hit. Bono was playing around with the lyrics until he internalized the exhilaration of the mix and belted out "It's a beautiful daaaay!" It had to stay, and another song had found its heart. "Stuck in a Moment You Can't Get Out Of" was written about Michael Hutchence. When Bono had heard the news of his death, he wrote the first draft of the song in a flash of anger and despair, determined that it not get too sentimental. He recalled:

> The greatest respect I could pay him was not to write some stupid, sentimental, soppy [expletive deleted] song.[11]

Edge had written a pop melody with a gospel flavor on the piano. They thought about bringing a choir in, but realized the four-member choir of Bono, Edge, Lanois, and Eno would do just fine. "Walk On" was written for Aung San Suu Kyi after Bono became inspired by her courage and the sacrifices she was continuing to endure in her ongoing struggle to bring democracy to Burma. The song contains the title of the album, "The only baggage you can bring/Is all that you can't leave behind." Lanois and Eno got tired of working on it and thought it should be left behind, but Bono believed in it. Eventually, Steve Lillywhite came in to mix it and it made the final cut. "Kite" became a song for Bono's father. He was feeling the presence of death, of his own mortality, and was eager to write some lasting testaments for his own kids to remember him by. Bono recalled:

> The spiritual journey was interesting to him. Because he wasn't a believer; he didn't believe in God towards the end. He was a Catholic, but he lost his faith along the way.[12]

"Peace on Earth" dances on the edge of a cynicism that U2 has rarely ever entertained. The Omagh bombing shook Bono to the core of his faith, and his vocal is twisted with bitterness and was the last thing to be recorded for the album. Eno had left and Mike Hedges, who had done a remix of "Numb" from *Zooropa,* came in to assist Lanois. They finished it up the night before the final album was delivered to the record company.

All That You Can't Leave Behind was a painstaking record to make, but they were driven to better themselves and recapture the relevancy they thought they'd lost with *Pop.* The cover was shot in the Paul Andreu-designed Roissy terminal in Charles De Gaulle Airport in Paris. It was Bono's idea to put up the Biblical passage "J33.3" on the digital clock. It refers to Jeremiah 33:3, which reads, "Call unto Me and I will answer you." Bono has called it "God's telephone number."[13] The "Beautiful Day" video was filmed on the airport runway with Jonas Akerlund directing. The image is of a band in motion, in transit, shuffling off the mortal coil of one world for the redemption of the next. The album was released on October 31, Larry's thirty-ninth birthday, and went straight to number one in 32 countries. In the United States, however, it was held off the number one spot by Jay-Z's *Roc La Familia.*

U2 immediately began a six-week promotional tour that included London, Paris, New York, Los Angeles, and Rio de Janeiro. They shot the video for "Walk On" with Akerlund while in Rio in November, and a week later in Los Angeles they shot the "Stuck in a Moment You Can't Get Out Of" video with Kevin Godley. In December, U2 made their first-ever appearance on *Saturday Night*

Live playing "Beautiful Day" and "Elevation." Joey Ramone came by to visit, and they reminisced about the old days playing old Ramones' covers around Dublin.

In February 2001, U2 won a surprising three Grammys. They thought the United States had lost interest after *Pop*, but they were wrong—the new album struck a chord with American audiences, reigniting the band's career. Bono declared U2 was reapplying for the job of best band in the world.[14] The awards marked not only a new-found fame, but also a new way of approaching the media and the commercial market. Whereas before they only gave a handful of interviews a year, now they were willing to do whatever came their way. Part of this had to do with the influence of the Internet, which was opening up possibilities for communicating with fans like never before. U2 realized that the competition had become very stiff and that if they didn't take advantage of opportunities then another band would.

U2 embarked on their new Elevation tour from March through June in the United States, and decided to stick to arenas after the experience of PopMart. Reviewers described the new record and tour as back to basics, and Willie Williams designed the austere, but evocative, heart-shaped stage. The band's appearance was also radically different. Gone were the cowboy hats and bubble pants of Pop-Mart in favor of T-shirts and industrial-washed jeans. U2 was determined not to repeat past mistakes or to overreach, and opening night in Miami on March 24 was abuzz with anticipation. After the Corrs finished their set, U2 mounted the stage with the house lights on, a gesture that would come to symbolize much of what the open-hearted tour was about. It took the band some time to hit their stride because they were out of practice and hadn't played live in three years. Bono went disappearing into the crowd and ran around the perimeter of the arena without letting the band know beforehand. Bono recalls:

> I really believe it is my job to attack the distance between performer and audience, from climbing speaker stacks to stage diving, it is all the same thought.[15]

In April, they found out Joey Ramone had died from cancer. A friend let them know his favorite song was "In a Little While," which he was listening to when he passed away in the hospital. For the rest of the tour they dedicated the song to him. Bono's fourth child—a son—was born in May. Soon after, Bono found out his father was dying. It was the first time anyone in the band had been faced with the imminent death of a family member. Bono got through by singing the songs night after night, imagining he was conversing with Bob in a way he never could. Bono spoke about debt relief at Harvard's annual Class Day ceremony in June, and he was awarded an honorary degree. He was throwing himself into his commitments in an attempt to hold back the inevitable loss of his last parent.

U2 kicked off their European tour on July 6 in Copenhagen, with the Stereophonics opening. During the European tour, Bono frequently flew home to be by his father's side. Toward the end Bob had Parkinson's disease, so they were not able to talk much. Bono read him Shakespeare and his older brother, Norm, took care of many of the logistics. For Bono it brought up memories of his mother's death, and feelings he thought he had escaped came flooding back.

In July, Bono attended the G8 Summit in Genoa, Italy. When violence broke out he condemned it, but admitted understanding the anger. On August 21, Bob Hewson died in the early morning with Bono by his side. His last words were "f*** off," after the nurse had asked him if he needed anything.[16] U2 was playing later in the day at London Earl's Court, and Bono wanted to finish the show—it was what Bob would have wanted. In his father's memory, he knelt and did the sign of the cross, explaining that he wrote "Kite" for his father and changing the lyrics from "the last of the rock stars" to "the last of the opera stars."

The day after the funeral on August 25, U2 took the stage at Slane Castle to Thin Lizzy's "The Boys Are Back in Town," playing their first of two nights for the first time in 20 years. During "One," an image of Bono's father was shown on the video screens as Bono sang a snippet of the Three Degrees' "When Will I See You Again." It was a very public way to grieve, and the rest of the band was deeply concerned for Bono's well-being. A week later, when they played their second show, it went much smoother, and although they filmed both performances they only used footage from the second. Later in September Bono went to Bali, Indonesia, with friend Simon Carmody to relax, and ended up trying to use booze to drown the grief he was feeling for his father.[17] While there he managed to write some lyrics, including "One Step Closer" and "Electrical Storm."[18]

At the beginning of September Bono organized a charity single of Marvin Gaye's "What's Going On" with more than 20 artists, including Britney Spears and Destiny's Child, taking part. U2 then took a month off, and Bono was in Venice when he walked into the American Hotel and saw that two planes had flown into the World Trade Center in New York City. U2 decided to go ahead with the U.S. fall tour, and all the shows sold out. The album picked up sales, and radio began playing it more often—it seemed to resonate on a deeper level after September 11. The songs were emotionally raw and wrestled with some big questions, all of which the public could identify with at the time.

The U.S. concerts were very volatile, with emotions on full display. Their first New York show took place in Madison Square Garden on October 24. Catherine Owens came up with the idea to roll all the names of the people who had died in the September 11 attacks during "Walk On." The house lights went on for "Where the Streets Have No Name," and Bono saw an entire audience with tears in their eyes. He told them they looked beautiful, and later included the image in "City of Blinding Lights." He recalled:

> These people were not statistics. We used these giant screens to project the names of everyone who'd lost their life. Everybody in Madison Square Garden could see somebody they knew or somebody who knew somebody, and the whole place wept.[19]

In November, they played *The Tonight Show with Jay Leno* for the first time; it was a special Thanksgiving performance in honor of the U.S. military. The Elevation tour ended on December 2 in Miami. While the band took time off, Edge and Bono attended to responsibilities beyond the immediate scope of U2. Edge paid tribute to Stuart Adamson, the guitarist with the Skids and Big Country, who had recently committed suicide. Both of Adamson's bands were influences on U2—the Skids for their rousing punk anthems like "The Saints Are Coming" and Big Country for their sweeping Celtic rock. Steve Lillywhite had produced both U2 and Big Country in the early 1980s, and the bands would often cross paths and join each other onstage to support one another. In early 2002, Bono attended the opening of the World Economic Forum in New York and sat on a panel with UN Secretary General Kofi Annan, Archbishop Desmond Tutu, Elie Weisel, and Queen Rania of Jordan. He later joined Bill Gates to announce the creation of DATA (Debt, Aid, Trade for Africa). Bono's profile was on the rise, and he was earning a reputation for being somewhat of an expert on debt relief issues as well as Africa and AIDS.

The band reconvened on February 3 to play the Super Bowl in New Orleans. U2 played a brief, 15-minute set at half time, and as "MLK" began the names of the 9/11 victims rolled down the video screen. It was a triumphant end to an emotionally draining tour. Later that month they were nominated again for eight Grammys and won four, including Best Song for "Walk On" and Best Rock album for *All That You Can't Leave Behind*. Around this time, they released a seven-track EP titled *7* that was only available through Target department stores in the United States. It included songs from *All That You Can't Leave Behind*'s singles including "Summer Rain," "Always," and "Big Girls Are Best."

Bono made the cover of the March 4 edition of *Time* magazine with the story "Can Bono Save The World?" focusing on his humanitarian work with Jubilee 2000 and the more recent DATA. With the tour finished, Bono was looking beyond the scope of the group more than ever before and was becoming recognized for it. Then at Easter, when he was in Eze, he finally found the relief he had been searching for since his father had become terminally ill:

> In this little church, on Easter morning, I just got down on my knees, and I let go of whatever anger I had against my father. And I thanked God for him being my father, and for the gifts that I have been given through him. And I let go of that. I wept, and I felt rid of it.[20]

NOTES

1. Assayas, 172.
2. McGee, 208.
3. "Grammys Beam Ray of Light on Female Artists." February 26, 1999. www .rollingstone.com: http://www.rollingstone.com/news/story/5927410/ grammys_beam_ray_of_light_on_female_artists (accessed April 29, 2009).
4. "Bono Inducts Bruce Springsteen—'99." March 15, 1999. www.u2_inter views.tripod.com/index.html: http://u2_interviews.tripod.com/id141.html (accessed April 29, 2009).
5. McGee, 213.
6. "Where Two Roads Meet—The Million Dollar Hotel, and All That You Can't Leave Behind." http://www.u2faqs.com/history/f.html#3. (accessed April 29, 2009).
7. Stokes, 143.

8. McGee, 217.
9. *U2 by U2*, 296.
10. Stokes, 147.
11. Ibid., 148.
12. Assayas, 24.
13. *U2 by U2*, 303.
14. Ibid., 303.
15. Ibid., 305.
16. Ibid., 307.
17. Assayas, 23.
18. McGee, 238.
19. Assayas, 196.
20. Ibid., 23.

CHAPTER NINE

One Step Closer: *How to Dismantle an Atomic Bomb* (2002–2006)

The Elevation tour left U2 feeling motivated and inspired. They often found it difficult to let the energy go at the end of a tour, so this time they directed it toward recording new material. They set up a space in Monte Carlo and began rehearsals for material to be used on their next record. They also wrote "The Hands That Built America" for Martin Scorsese's film *Gangs Of New York*. The song was nominated for an Oscar, but lost to Eminem's "Lose Yourself" for Best Song.

In March, Bono appeared with President George W. Bush at the White House to announce $5 billion to help fight poverty in Africa. As they strolled across the White House grounds Bono waved and flashed a peace sign. Like a good lobbyist, Bono had been making inroads into the Bush administration and looking for ways to further the cause of debt relief. In May, he began an 11-day tour of the African countries Ghana, South Africa, Uganda, and Ethiopia with U.S. Treasury Secretary Paul O'Neill. At each stop, Bono pressed the secretary for more U.S. aid, and his lobbying eventually paid off. In the State of the Union address in January 2003, Bush announced another $15 billion dollars over 15 years to fight AIDS in Africa.

Around this time, U2 began work on a new song, "Electrical Storm" with William Orbit, a producer and protégé of Brian Eno. The song was Bono's attempt to express what he had felt in the

United States—a sense of dread and nervous anticipation in the wake of 9/11. They shot the video in Eze, near Bono's home, and the song was released at the end of August 2002. Eze was becoming a home away from home for the band; its warm climate and easy pace were a welcome change from Dublin. In June, Edge and Morleigh got married at a ceremony on a hilltop overlooking the Cote d'Azur, with Bono as best man and the whole band in attendance.

After a summer of rest and relaxation, Bono popped up in Chicago to duet on "It's Only Rock and Roll (But I Like It)" with Mick Jagger and the Rolling Stones. He had previously contributed vocals to "Joy" from Jagger's 2001 solo album, *Goddess in the Doorway,* and the two had solidified their friendship. Bono also appeared on the *Oprah Winfrey Show* and was now able to embrace the confessional of the daytime talk shows he once had mocked. In the meantime, Edge told *Hot Press* that U2 would have an album out the next year and that three tracks were already done—"Sometimes You Can't Make it on Your Own," "Original of Species," and "All Because of You." U2's *Best of 1990–2000* was released in November, and later that month Bono was honored by the Simon Wiesenthal Center. Founder Rabbi Marvin Hier said Bono was "fulfilling the prophetic vision of 'tikkun olam'—to help repair the world and leave it in better condition than when we found it."[1]

On December 23, the rock community was shocked and saddened when Joe Strummer died suddenly of a heart attack. At the time of his death, he was working with Bono and Dave Stewart on a song titled "46664 (Long Walk to Freedom)" for a future Nelson Mandela charity concert.[2] The Clash had an enormous influence on U2, and Bono was always drawn to Strummer's outspoken political views. They had been one of the most political bands of the British punk explosion, even titling their 1980 album *Sandinista!* in support of the Nicaraguan revolutionary government, and *Rolling Stone* had chosen *London Calling* as the best album of the 1980s. Throughout their early career, U2's sound often drew comparisons to the Clash, and while they were recording *War* Bono often pressed Edge to recreate their signature guitar sound. Bono said: "The Clash was the greatest rock band. They wrote the rule book for U2. It's such a shock."[3]

Every year before the Grammys, MusiCares honors a musician who has made a significant contribution to music and been active in works of philanthropy. In February 2003 it was Bono's turn. The event turned out to be a star-studded affair with Michael Stipe, Norah Jones, David Bowie, Bill Clinton, and Aretha Franklin in attendance. At one point, Elvis Costello exclaimed from the stage, "give him the f***ing Nobel Peace Prize now!"[4] Later the same month, French President Jacques Chirac awarded Bono the Chevalier of Legion of Honor, France's highest civilian award.

At the end of May, Bono turned up at the Pavarotti and Friends concert in Modena, Italy, to perform "One" and duet with Pavarotti on "Ave Maria." The concert raised £1 million for Iraqi war refugees. Bono had written new lyrics addressing the war that had recently broken out:

And strength is not without humility
It's weakness, an untreatable disease
And war is always the choice
Of the chosen who will not have to fight[5]

In the summer, at his Malibu home in California, Edge began woodshedding some guitar ideas and came up with the monster riff that would form the basis for U2's next big song, "Vertigo." Bono loved what he heard, and could tell Edge wanted to make a guitar record. The band gathered to talk about the new album and agreed it should be based around the four of them, like *All That You Can't Leave Behind* had been, but they wanted it to be harder and more up-tempo. Bands like the White Stripes, Green Day, and the Strokes had brought the guitar back in vogue, and U2 wanted to be part of it. They started kicking around names of producers, and Chris Thomas came up. He had an impressive pedigree and had worked with everyone from the Beatles and Sex Pistols to Roxy Music.

They contacted Thomas, he said he was interested, and they set a date for February to go into Hanover Quay studios, but soon things began to turn sour. U2 usually began recording without finished songs, and it could be difficult for producers to adapt. Despite tensions, by the summer of 2003 they thought they had an album's worth of material. Bono was ready to release it, but Larry and Adam resisted, feeling the tunes just weren't good enough. Bono backed off and agreed to wait a little longer. He has said that U2's songwriting process is often an accidental one, and the better they get at it, the harder it is for them to conjure up their unique magic.[6] In late October, U2 spent a week at London's Air Studios with Thomas. They brought in a 50-piece orchestra for one session, but it turned out to be a disaster; Thomas felt it was one of his worst days ever with a band.[7] Daniel Lanois was invited to listen to the album and ended up contributing pedal steel to the meditative, "One Step Closer."

At the end of November Edge and Bono flew to Cape Town, South Africa, for a break and to clear their minds. They performed "One" and the classic "Unchained Melody" at the 46664 concert in tribute to Nelson Mandela, and afterward Bono attended Pavarotti and Nicoletta Mantovani's wedding in Modena, Italy. He sang "All I Want Is You," changing the lyrics to "When the pasta has run dry/And the wine no longer gets you high/ All I want is you."[8]

When the band reunited back in Dublin, they found themselves in need of a second opinion on the new material. In January, Steve Lillywhite was invited to offer some perspective, and he ended up staying for over six months. When he heard what they had done, he agreed with Larry and Adam—the songs were missing that special U2 spark. He leveled with the band, explaining that the material just wasn't up to the quality it should be. Bono and Edge swallowed hard and went back to work. The release date was pushed back not a few months, but almost a year.

After Lillywhite joined, the sessions picked up with a new spirit of optimism. He had the band set up in a brighter and bigger room to change the ambience and mood. U2 went back to work, and while Bono was away receiving an award from the King Center in Atlanta they recorded "Vertigo," "Crumbs from Your Table," All Because of You," and "Original of the Species." Bono added the vocals later. The band was being influenced once again by an invasion of Iraq, just as they had been a decade earlier during the Persian Gulf War. The lingering fear of a terrorist attack in the wake of 9/11 and the Bali and Madrid bombings contributed to a sense of danger that the band picked up on. *How to Dismantle an Atomic Bomb* seemed like an appropriate title that captured the spirit of the times. Bono said, "Someone who's paranoid, in my opinion, is a person in full possession of the facts."[9] He also suggested that the title referred to coming to terms with the death of his father.

Garrett "Jacknife" Lee, a keyboard player and producer of Snow Patrols' breakthrough album, *Final Straw,* was brought in by Lillywhite to help out. Lee had a knack for taking an ordinary song and adding a twist to make it more interesting. The band was spending a lot of time on the material, building up the songs and taking them apart to examine their component parts. Bono was away for much of this time, and his absence allowed the others to focus solely on the music.

The first version of "Vertigo" began as "Native Son"; it was about Leonard Peltier, the activist and member of the American Indian Movement (AIM) who was convicted and sentenced in 1977 for the murder of two FBI Agents. Bono believed, along with many others, that Peltier's trial was compromised and regarded him as a political prisoner. The lyric then evolved into a Spanish-inflected song called "Shark Soup," at which point it picked up its erroneous intro, "Unos, dos, tres, catorces! (One, two, three, fourteen!)" Bono ultimately settled on the final version about "a disused soul in a well-used nightclub."[10] The song also offered a nod back to their origins with a quote from "Stories For Boys"—"hello, hello."

"Sometimes You Can't Make It on Your Own" had been around since before Bono's father died, and he had sung a version of it at his funeral in 2001. Lillywhite thought something was missing, and one day he pushed Bono to add the falsetto bridge on the spot—"It's you when I look in the mirror." The final version is remarkable, uncovering the kernel of human pathos recognizable to anyone who has suffered the loss of a loved one. As Bono says on the CD's accompanying DVD, "a song can change the world . . . it can change the temperature in the room." For someone who spent the better part of his career addressing the loss of his mother, this was something new. Bono opens up directly to his father telling him, "You're the reason I sing/You're the reason why the opera is in me." It's an explosive confession that raises the room temperature, and for Bono's father, who loved opera, it's a fitting tribute. It went on to win a Grammy for Best Song in 2006.

"City of Blinding Lights" was a leftover from the *Pop* sessions. Bono added a lyric after he witnessed the audience in tears at the New York concert in 2001. Around this time, Bono attended Anton Corbijn's exhibition in the Netherlands called *U2 and I: The Photographs 1982–2004*. While looking at an image of himself as a much younger man of 21, he was struck by the expression on his face. It was that same feeling of wide-open wonder that he wanted to capture with "City of Blinding Lights." Seeing the photo brought to mind the changes he had experienced:

> I realized how much I'd lost. I'm not talking about lines on my face or a thicker head of hair but that way of looking at the world. There was such clarity to it, but it was so defiant in a way.[11]

Edge and Bono wrote the music for "Crumbs from Your Table" while blotto in France. The lyric reflects the work Bono was doing with

DATA and the frustration of dealing with indifferent governments and institutions like the church. Bono expressed the absurdity of how the location where you might reside could determine "whether you live or whether you die." It is this conviction that has fueled much of Bono's drive to alleviate "stupid poverty":

> "Crumbs From Your Table" is one of the most vicious songs ever. It's full of spleen about the church and its refusal to hear God's voice on the AIDS emergency.[12]

"Original of the Species" was written for Edge's daughter Hollie and addresses the self-esteem issues many teenagers wrestle with. As Bono said:

> I'm just saying to them "you are one of a kind, you're an original of the species." So it's a "Be who you are" song.[13]

"Yahweh" was how Moses addressed God when confronted with the burning bush in the Old Testament. Bono said, "It's not meant to be spoken, but I got around it by singing it. I hope I don't offend anyone."[14] "Yahweh" is an anthem of renewal born from the ashes of 9/11, with U2 beseeching God to answer the question many still had in 2004: "Why the dark before the dawn?"

The album was finally finished in early July 2004. A few nights before the sessions ended, they revisited a song that included a lyric of the album's title. Bono wanted to get the phrase back on the album, and the song turned into "Fast Cars"; it ended up as a bonus track on albums released in Britain and Japan. U2 was very excited about the new material and felt it was their strongest, but maybe not quite their most innovative, to date. The cover harkened back to the black, white, and red of their 1980s albums. There was much discussion over the title, with some dissenting views, but Bono's vision prevailed. After wrapping up in Dublin, U2 went to Nice, France, to do a photo shoot and some interviews. Edge had an early CD of the album and was listening to it on a portable sound system when it went missing. Universal, their record company, was not amused. They contacted Interpol and opened a huge investigation to prevent it from leaking on the Internet. In the end, nothing came of it and it never surfaced.

At the end of July, Bono and Ali appeared in Boston for the Democratic Party convention. They attended a tribute in the evening for Senator Ted Kennedy, and Bono performed "Pride" and "The

Hands That Built America" with help from Yo-Yo Ma and the Boston Pops Orchestra. Later, in September, he popped up at the Republican Party convention in New York and was interviewed by Fox News' Bill O'Reilly; Bono said he was not "rooting" for any presidential candidate. Bono was worried about appearing to be partisan and knew that for the purposes of DATA he might have to work with either party to get what was needed. For some, however, his unwillingness to take sides came across as disingenuous, even cowardly. Some people thought it had more to do with his business connections than anything else. Bono's lobbying took a more partisan angle in Britain when, at the Labour Conference in September, he praised Tony Blair and Gordon Brown for their efforts to fight AIDS in Africa.

Back in U2-land, Paul had been working on developing new strategies to market the album. The band had had a relationship with Apple since 2002, they were one of the first adopters of iTunes, and an idea was hatched for U2 to participate in Apple's fall campaign selling iPods. U2 wouldn't get paid for it; instead they received a royalty on every U2 iPod sold. In October, Apple premiered two commercials featuring U2's new single, "Vertigo," promoting iTunes, the iPod, and the new album.

When Bono was in Portland speaking at the World Affairs Council, two women came forward to return the personal belongings he had misplaced back in 1981. After all the years, the truth could finally be told—no one had ever stolen Bono's notebook; he had left it behind! In November, Bono received another blast from the past when Bob Geldof and Midge Ure reassembled a new clutch of pop stars to form Band Aid 20 for an updated version of the single, "Do They Know It's Christmas?" Bono joined Paul McCartney and George Michael as the only members from the original 1984 session. There was a bit of a kafuffle when Justin Hawkins from the Darkness tried to sing Bono's original lyric until Bono, or maybe Paul and U2 incorporated, insisted he do it himself.[15]

How To Dismantle an Atomic Bomb was released on November 22 and became U2's fastest-selling CD ever, just weeks after George W. Bush was elected in what *Rolling Stone*'s Rob Sheffield called "another four-year moment" the United States couldn't get out of. The magazine gave the album 4 out of 5 stars, noting the band had "trimmed the Euro-techno pomp, sped up the tempos and let the Edge define the songs with his revitalized guitar."[16] To promote the album, U2 shot a video for "All Because of You," directed by Phil Joanou, on the back of a flatbed truck driving through the streets of

Manhattan. The same afternoon U2 played a 45-minute free concert for MTV in Brooklyn's Empire-Fulton Ferry State Park.

They were gearing up for a yearlong tour when news arrived in December that Edge's seven-year-old daughter, Sian, had come down with leukemia. Everything was put on hold as he returned to his family. Lawyers representing Edge contacted a number of media outlets to ask that they not publish any details about which family member was ill. The *Sunday World* refused to comply and went ahead with their story.[17] After much discussion, Edge was able to find a way to commit to the tour while also looking after his family. Paul had to rebook the U.S. tour and reschedule it for a month later to allow enough flexibility for Edge to return to his Los Angeles home as frequently as possible. As a result, U2 was unable to play as many dates. When tickets went on sale through the band's Web site, a fiasco ensued and Larry later issued an online letter of apology. Fans who were promised access to highly valued seats found they were unable to make any bookings and lost out to others. Larry's letter included a jab at "so-called U2 fans" who were accusing the band of cheating them, signing off with, "I've only got two words for you . . . ."[18]

In February 2005, rehearsals began in Mexico with Edge playing more intensely than ever. Sian's illness had caused him to reorder all his priorities and stay focused on what mattered. He began introducing songs from *Boy* with its theme of innocence, and it seemed appropriate juxtaposed with the new album's darker songs about poverty, war, and mortality. At the Grammys, Bono joined Billie Joe Armstrong, Steve Tyler, and others on the Beatles' "Across the Universe" for the 200,000 victims who had died in the Indian Ocean tsunami at the end of December 2004. Adam was in Thailand at the time, but had escaped unharmed. U2 won three awards at the ceremonies, including Best Rock Song for "Vertigo," and Edge dedicated his award to Sian. With 17 Grammy Awards, U2 was now tied for eighth on the list of all-time winners.

Bruce Springsteen inducted U2 into the Rock and Roll Hall of Fame in March, joining the Pretenders, Ojays, Buddy Guy, and Percy Sledge. He had been an early supporter of the band, and they shared a mutual passion for performing. Springsteen said:

> U2 has not only evened the odds but they've beaten them by continuing to do their finest work and remaining at the top of their game and the charts for 25 years. I feel a great affinity for these guys as people as well as musicians.[19]

U2 performed four songs, including a version of "I Still Haven't Found What I'm Looking For," with Springsteen.

Multimedia artist Catherine Owens began working on a way to incorporate the Universal Declaration of Human Rights with African flags into the show without it overshadowing the music. Bono also came across a symbol—COEXIST—developed by the Polish artist Piotr Mlodozeniec, that blended the Islamic crescent for C, the Jewish Star of David for X, and Christian cross for the T. He began wearing it as a bandana, and it was added into the video display. Around this time, DATA had started a new campaign called "One," and Bono began making a speech of varying lengths about its aims. Some nights Larry grimaced and yawned behind his kit when it seemed Bono would go on forever. When they arrived in Chicago, U2 shot a video at the United Center on Bono's birthday. He later joined Coldplay's Chris Martin and Gwyneth Paltrow for a big bash. A week later, at New York's Slipper Room, U2 performed with Leonard Cohen on a video for "Tower of Song" for the upcoming tribute film *I'm Your Man.*

In the run-up to the G8 Summit in Gleneagles, Scotland, Bono was giving more interviews and attending more meetings. His commitments often caused him to leave the tour, and Paul was worried about the condition of his voice. Bono was putting in very long days, but it wasn't affecting the quality of his performances. He was appearing everywhere and with some disturbing reminders of the architects of the Iraq War—President Bush and Prime Minister Blair, for example. It was a tough call—Larry was the one member who had joined an antiwar rally in Dublin and despised the politicians Bono was appearing with. But Bono felt strongly that July's G8 Summit could prove to be a game changer for debt relief. There had been discussions about staging another Live Aid concert, but Bob Geldof was never interested. Finally, after much prodding, he agreed at the last minute and the scramble was on to organize the event. The official announcement was made on May 31, with only six weeks to book the acts.

U2 headed over to Europe and kicked off the next leg of the tour on June 10 for 60,000 fans in Brussels. The energy at these outdoor shows was incredible, and U2 felt they were playing to the best crowds of their career. Then, on July 2, U2 opened Live 8 with Paul McCartney in London's Hyde Park, performing "Sgt. Pepper's Lonely Hearts Club Band." The lyrics were actually true—"It was twenty years ago today . . ." since the first Live Aid concert in 1985. Within

45 minutes the song was made available on iTunes, eventually making the *Guinness Book of World Records* for the quickest single to be put on sale. U2 also played three of their own: "Beautiful Day," "Vertigo," and "One."

Immediately following their performance, U2 had to fly to Vienna to play another gig on the same day. A few days later, in Katowice, Poland, when U2 started into "New Year's Day" the audience surprised the band by using flash cards to make the red and white colors of the Polish flag. It was their way of thanking the band for remembering them during the Solidarity struggle back in 1983 when the Iron Curtain was still up. Bono continued flying back to the G8 Summit to meet with world leaders. It was rough on his voice, and he was not getting enough sleep, but in the end DATA received the $50 billion it had requested for Africa.

U2 was in Berlin when the London bombings occurred on July 7. It was a harrowing reminder of the threat terrorism still posed, and they dedicated "Running to Stand Still" to the victims and their families. In September, the band arrived in Toronto to rehearse for the third leg of the Vertigo tour a few days after Hurricane Katrina hit New Orleans. Edge began talking with producer Bob Ezrin and decided to help the musicians who had lost their livelihoods by hooking up with Gibson guitars to provide assistance.

The tour opened on September 12 in the Air Canada Center in Toronto, and Daniel Lanois joined them onstage as Leonard Cohen looked on in the audience. During their fifth show, local band Menew were invited on stage to play the first half of "Out of Control" with U2's instruments. A few days later Bono joined Eddie Vedder and Pearl Jam on Neil Young's "Rockin' in the Free World." In Philadelphia, Bruce Springsteen hopped onstage for Curtis Mayfield's "People Get Ready." Bono teased the crowd, saying he didn't know the lyrics and needed some help as Springsteen strolled on the stage and picked up Bono's Falcon guitar. At the end of October, U2 won the four awards it was nominated for from *Billboard*—Top Tour, Top Draw, Top Boxscore, and Top Manager (for Principle Management).

Bono wrote the essay "This Generation's Moon Shot" for *Time Magazine*'s November 1 issue, spelling out the benefits of defeating diseases like malaria and tuberculosis. In Las Vegas, Mary J. Blige sang "One" with the band, and Brandon Flowers from the Killers joined them on "In a Little While." U2 then announced that the tour would continue through 2006 to Mexico, South America, Australia, New Zealand, and Japan.

Edge took some time out to tour New Orleans and launch the formation of the charity Music Rising to help musicians who had lost their instruments and livelihoods in Hurricane Katrina. Later, in New York, one of the band's very first inspirations, Patti Smith, joined them on John Lennon's "Instant Karma." At their gig in Montreal, Lanois was invited onstage again for "Bad," and at the next show Arcade Fire joined the band for a frenetic version of Joy Division's "Love Will Tear Us Apart." U2 closed the tour in Portland on December 19 with Kanye West and returned to Dublin for the holidays.

In December, *Time* magazine named Bono and Bill and Melinda Gates as their Persons of the Year for 2005. It was a huge accomplishment and helped build momentum not only for DATA, but for U2 as well. In February 2006, Bono delivered the keynote address representing DATA at the 51st annual National Prayer Breakfast, attended by President George Bush. He focused on debt relief, saying:

> Preventing the poorest of the poor from selling their products while we sing the virtues of the free market, that's not charity: That's a justice issue. Holding children to ransom for the debts of their grandparents, that's not charity: That's a justice issue. Withholding lifesaving medicines out of deference to the Office of Patents, well that's not charity. To me, that's a justice issue.[20]

At the end of the month U2 appeared at the Grammys, collecting five more awards including Album and Song of the Year. It was a fitting end to a year that had seen U2 scale the heights of their creative powers again, 30 years after they had met in Larry's kitchen.

NOTES

1. "'Beautiful Day' for Bono." November 22, 2002. www.atu2.com: http://www.atu2.com/news/article.src?ID=2678&Key=earns&Year=2002 (accessed April 29, 2009).
2. "46664 (Long Walk to Freedom)." http://www.u2wanderer.org/disco/dalb016.html (accessed April 29, 2009).
3. "Clash star Strummer dies." December 27, 2002. http://news.bbc.co.uk/2/hi/entertainment/2600669.stm (accessed April 29, 2009).
4. McGee, 255.
5. Ibid., 258.
6. Ibid., 261.

7. *U2 by U2*, 318.
8. McGee, 263.
9. Ibid., 265.
10. Stokes, 171.
11. *U2 by U2*, 322.
12. *U2 by U2*, 324.
13. Stokes, 179.
14. Ibid., 182.
15. "Bono sings famous Band Aid Line." November 17, 2004. news.bbc.co.uk: http://news.bbc.co.uk/2/hi/entertainment/4012573.stm (accessed April 29, 2009)
16. "Album Review: U2's *How To Dismantle an Atomic Bomb*." December 4, 2004. www.rollingstone.com: http://www.rollingstone.com/reviews/album/6629835/review/6630492/howtodismantleanatomicbomb (accessed April 29, 2009).
17. McGee, 279-280.
18. Ibid., 281.
19. "Bruce Springsteen Inducts U2 into the Rock and Roll Hall of Fame." March 17, 2005. www.u2station.com: http://www.u2station.com/news/archives/2005/03/transcript_bruc.php (accessed April 29, 2009).
20. "Bono: Keynote Address at the 54th National Prayer Breakfast." February 2, 2006. /www.americanrhetoric.com: http://www.americanrhetoric.com/speeches/bononationalprayerbreakfast.htm (accessed April 29, 2009).

CHAPTER TEN

Hope & History: *No Line on the Horizon* (2006–)

After speaking at the 2006 Davos economic conference, launching PRODUCT(RED), and picking up five Grammys for *How To Dismantle an Atomic Bomb*, Bono joined Ali to promote their new clothing line, Edun. "Nude" spelled backwards, Edun was launched in 2005 with Irish designer Rogan Gregory to foster employment and trade in developing countries, especially sub-Saharan Africa.

In February, U2 kicked off the South America leg of the *Vertigo* tour at the Tecnologico Stadium in Monterrey, Mexico, with the Secret Machines. In Brazil, Bono met with President Lula da Silva to discuss poverty issues, and the band later attended Rio's Carnaval. Bono was awarded the Pablo Neruda merit award in Chile, the country's highest honor for the arts, from President Ricardo Lagos. Later that day, U2 received Amnesty International's 2005 Ambassador of Conscience Award at the Estadio Nacional, the same location where former dictator Augusto Pinochet had detained, tortured, and killed his opponents. When they reached Buenos Aires, U2 met the Mothers of the Plaza De Mayo and performed "Mothers of the Disappeared" in their honor before meeting soccer legend Diego Maradona.

Bono appeared via video at the *NME* awards to present Bob Geldof with the Hero of the Year. Bono and Geldof go back a long way. Both hail from the Dublin area and fronted bands with international aspirations in the days when Ireland's chief exports were

Guinness and Thin Lizzy. Although nine years Bono's senior, Geldof was a well-known figure in the Dublin scene of the late 1970s as the front man for the Boomtown Rats. Later they discovered a mutual passion for Africa, joining forces at various points during the past 25 years to eradicate poverty with Live Aid, and, more recently, debt relief. Bono delivered a humorous speech, making use of one of Geldof's pet phrases:

> I'm so very pleased that upon asking Bob to do Live 8, we did not listen when he told us to f*** off. And I hope he is too. Because a cheque worth 50 billion dollars has been signed for the poorest people on the planet. Every time somebody buys one of these Live 8 DVDs we'll put pressure on the politicians to cash the cheque. Thank you very much for this award. And to my friend who is picking it up in all our honor: F***. Off."[1]

After the South American tour wrapped up, Bono and his family flew to Sydney for a short vacation before beginning the Australian shows. Then, suddenly, the band was forced to postpone the tour after Edge's daughter took a turn for the worse. U2 announced that the tour would resume later that year in November. In the meantime, the band found things to keep themselves occupied. Bono helped kick off a Samuel Beckett Centenary Festival in Dublin, declaring himself a fan. He recalled giving Beckett a copy of *The Unforgettable Fire* back in 1985, but wasn't sure he had ever listened to it. In April, he discovered that Italian Prime Minister Silvio Berlusconi had been using his image in a political brochure. Bono wrote a letter saying he felt "exploited" and published it on the front page of Italy's *Corriere della Sera* newspaper. He also used the opportunity to remind Berlusconi about the pledge he had made to cancel the debt of developing countries. Adam got engaged to his long-time Canadian girlfriend, Susie Smith, but within a year they had split. The couple had met 10 years before when she was working at Principle Management in Dublin as an assistant to Paul. Edge appeared at a fund-raiser for Hillary Clinton in Beverly Hills, and then surfaced in New Orleans at the Jazzfest, joining Dave Mathews to raise money for the victims of Hurricane Katrina. His daughter's condition had stabilized, and he was spending most of his time in the United States, where her doctor was.

In May, the sports network ESPN began airing four U2 commercials featuring their voice-overs promoting the upcoming World

Cup in Germany. The theme was "One Game Changes Everything."
In an ad about the Ivory Coast, Bono said:

> It's a simple thing. Just a ball and a goal. That simple thing . . .
> closes the schools, closes the shops, closes a city and stops a war.
> After three years of civil war, feuding factions talked for the first
> time in years and the president called a truce because the Ivory
> Coast qualified for its first-ever World Cup.[2]

Soon after, Bono was invited to edit an issue of the UK newspaper
The Independent. When it appeared on May 16 its cover was colored
red and it featured an image created by artist Damien Hirst announcing, "No News Today: Just 6,500 Africans died today as the result of
a preventable, treatable disease. (HIV/AIDS)." It included interviews
with Tony Blair, Gordon Brown, and Edge about his relief efforts in
New Orleans. Half the funds raised were donated to the Global Fund
to Fight AIDS. Afterward, Bono began a 10-day tour of the African
countries Lesotho, Rwanda, Tanzania, Nigeria, Mali, and Ghana as a
representative of DATA. He cropped his hair short, and a new
scheme was launched to encourage workers in the textile industry to
take an HIV test. He also met with Rwandan President Paul
Kagame.

Back in Dublin, Edge unveiled a bronze replica of Rory Gallagher's paint-stripped Fender Stratocaster in the Temple Bar district
in June. Edge had always been a fan, often citing Gallagher's "Blister
on the Moon" as the song that inspired him to master the guitar.
Around this time, Bono joined Sting, Nick Cave, and other artists by
contributing a song to the double album, *Rogue's Gallery: Pirate Ballads, Sea Songs & Chanteys,* that Johnny Depp organized to coincide
with the release of his film, *Pirates of the Caribbean II.* "A Dying Sailor
to His Shipmates" is a haunting dirge with Bono, accompanied by
accordion and fiddle, evoking Shane MacGowan's early work with
the Pogues.

U2 then made an application to the city to build a huge apart-
ment complex in Sir John Rogerson's Quay in Dublin's south docklands. The band's plan called for three eight-story buildings with 90
apartments. After 30 years together, the band had become much
more than a musical entity—they were now a global corporation.
They were also seeking ways to maximize their profits, but they
attracted some fierce criticism when they moved their royalties to the
Netherlands to avoid paying Irish taxes. People couldn't believe U2

was behaving like sordid tax evaders, even after the band defended the action by saying they paid taxes all over the world and that there was nothing illegal about what they were doing. In fact, they claimed everyone else in their financial bracket did the same thing. The band didn't seem to understand that "doing it because everyone else did" was part of the problem. U2 had never done anything just because others did. They were the exception, the true believers who had always blazed their own trail, but now they were copying a business model adopted by corporate rockers the Rolling Stones, who had operations based in Amsterdam since the early 1970s. As the story gathered momentum the band received harsher criticism, as did Bono when his private equity firm, Elevation Partners, bought a stake in *Forbes* magazine, which was owned by conservative businessman Steve Forbes. In another business-savvy move, U2 sold its Live Nation stock as part of a 12-year contract with the company when the world economy worsened in 2008.[3]

In September, U2 entered Abbey Road studios in London to work on their next album with Rick Rubin producing. Rubin had worked with Johnny Cash, the Red Hot Chili Peppers and the Beastie Boys and had a reputation for pulling out the best performances from the artists he worked with. U2 invited Green Day to record a cover of Scottish punkers the Skids' 1978 song, "The Saints Are Coming." The two bands had met before the Grammys in February at the Chateau Marmont in LA to discuss the possibility of playing together. To warm up, they banged out covers by the Buzzcocks and Stiff Little Fingers, and then decided to record with both bands' drummers and bass players, a full tilt musical assault. They also tried to recreate the iconic Beatles' *Abbey Road* photo outside the studio at the crosswalk.

On September 25, 2006, U2 and Green Day played an NFL pregame performance at the official reopening of the Superdome in New Orleans before the Saints' first home game since Hurricane Katrina. The performance began with Edge joining Green Day on "When September Ends," followed by the rest of U2 on a medley that included "House of the Rising Sun," "The Saints Are Coming," and "Beautiful Day." The game against the Atlanta Falcons was the second-most-watched cable television broadcast ever, attracting nearly 15 million viewers. The song was later included on a U2 compilation released in November.

Around this time, Bono and Ali flew to New York to launch Edun's new "ONE" T-shirts. They were made in Africa with local cotton, and $10 from every sale went to fight AIDS. The event included a speech by economist Jeffrey Sachs and a performance by Irish singer-songwriter Damian Rice. Bono lost his patience with the loud audience, telling them to take their "f***ing finger food and f*** off."[4] The band then appeared together in London to promote their huge coffee table book, *U2 by U2,* an autobiography written in their own words with old Mount Temple friend Neil McCormick. It was the band's attempt to set the record straight about their career, and included some rare photos and firsthand interviews. Harper-Collins was fully behind the release, printing half a million copies in 10 languages.

In October, Bono appeared in Chicago with Oprah Winfrey doing some early Christmas shopping to promote PRODUCT(RED). He was a guest on her TV show the next day with Alicia Keys, and together they performed "Don't Give Up (Africa)." Then he had to return to Dublin and spend three-and-a-half hours in the witness box over two days fighting to get his belongings back from his former stylist, Lola Cashman. U2 alleged she stole them, but Cashman countered that the items, estimated to be worth $7,300, had been gifts during U2's 1987 Joshua Tree tour. Why would the band go to so much trouble for so little, people wondered. Some speculated that they were angered by a book she wrote in 2003—*Inside the Zoo with U2*—that was panned as a sensationalistic attempt to cash in on their success. A month later U2 won the case, and Cashman was forced to return the items.

U2 decided to end their long-standing relationship with Island and prepared to release their next album, *U218 Singles,* a greatest hits package, through Mercury Records in time for the resumption of the Vertigo tour in Australia. They opened the tour in Brisbane on November 7 with Bono calling for the release of terrorist suspect David Hicks from Guantanamo Bay prison. He still enjoyed stirring the pot, and in an interview in Adelaide he said:

> The rock stars are all too cool. And I don't want to be that, I've gotten a bit too cool. I want to be like I was as a kid, I want to stay hot and passionate rather than cool.[5]

As though to illustrate this, he joined Kylie Minogue in Sydney, filling in for Robbie Williams on the hit song "Kids" during her comeback tour after she recovered from breast cancer. U2 was in town playing three nights at the Telstra Stadium, and Minogue was supposed to return the favor the next day, but had to cancel due to exhaustion.

U2 appeared with Pearl Jam, Paul Kelly, and others for the Make Poverty History concert in Melbourne. The event was timed to coincide with the G20 Summit being hosted by Australia, with the aim to raise public awareness. U2 and Pearl Jam joined forces as "UJAM" on Neil Young's "Rockin' in the Free World," which included some of Bono's adlibbed lyrics. At one point he sang, "You gotta trust your vision over visibility," a line that would show up almost three years later on "Moment of Surrender." There was speculation that Bono would meet Prime Minister John Howard, but plans fell through when Howard rejected Bono's request for a serious discussion about global aid, saying he didn't accept "preconditions" from anyone. Bono later met Australian Treasurer Peter Costello for a discussion on the issue.[6]

In Auckland, New Zealand, U2 played "One Tree Hill" for the first time since 1990, in honor of Greg Carroll. Bono made a plea for a tree to be replanted on the summit of Maungakiekie, the original Maori name for One Tree Hill. In Japan, Bono met with Prime Minister Shinzo Abe to discuss poverty and health issues in developing countries, especially Africa. The two hit it off, and Bono presented Abe with some Armani shades from the PRODUCT(RED) campaign. Later, in 2008, Bono returned to Japan for a speech to some 800 university students at Keio University, encouraging aid to Africa. While in Japan, U2 premiered their new track, "Window in the Skies." The video, directed by Gary Koepke, was made with a montage of U2's favorite artists, including the Beatles and Frank Sinatra, who were digitally altered to make it look like they were singing the lyrics.

The Vertigo tour wrapped up December 9 at Honolulu's Aloha Stadium with Pearl Jam and Green Day's Billie Joe Armstrong. It ended up being the second-highest-grossing tour ever, behind the Rolling Stones' A Bigger Bang Tour. The band took a break and Bono traveled to the Sundance Film Festival to support Julien Temple's new film, *Joe Strummer: The Future Is Unwritten*. He also appeared again at the Davos World Economic Forum and in a videotaped tribute at the Ireland Music Awards presenting Clannad with a lifetime achievement award. In March he received an award on behalf of the NAACP in Los Angeles and delivered a rousing speech in tribute, in part, to Martin Luther King Jr.

Around this time, the PRODUCT(RED) campaign began attracting some criticism. Its appeal for conspicuous consumption spurred a parody by a group of San Francisco designers and artists who responded with a Web site called buylesscrap.org. Co-creator of the site, Ben Davis, said, "The Red campaign proposes consumption as the cure to the world's evils. Can't we just focus on the real solution—giving money?"[7]

Bono was used to the criticism—it came with the territory as a global celebrity, and he had learned long ago to not let it get in his way. Instead, he wrote another essay for *Time* magazine called "A Time For Miracles" on the 50th anniversary of the Treaty of Rome. He evoked the "very human miracle" of how a united Europe found the capacity to forgive and build a new continent with the help of the Marshall Plan. That was the type of effort that was now needed to help Africa, he explained. Referring to the Irish word *meitheal,* meaning "helping each other when the work is the hardest," he exhorted developed nations to live up to their values and commit to helping the poorest of the poor.[8] It was this type of dedication to helping those less fortunate that earned Bono an honorary knighthood from the Queen. He showed up at the British ambassador's residence in Dublin with Ali, their four children, Edge, and Adam. His new title was Knight Commander of the Most Excellent Order of the British Empire (KBE). He said it would help him get more attention for his charity work and open up a few more doors.

In the United States, preacher Sarah Dylan Breuer had begun the U2charist, an event that consisted of a liturgical service featuring U2 songs such as "All I Want Is You, "40," and "I Still Haven't Found What I'm Looking For," and a message about God's call to rally around the Millennium Development Goals. Some fans were concerned about its explicitly religious overtones, but Bono said he didn't mind if U2's songs were in the church or on the street as long as the message was heard. Since beginning in 2003 the U2charist has spread around the world, drawing crowds in such disparate places as Hong Kong and Mexico City.

With their time off, Bono and Edge decided to write the music and lyrics for *Spiderman: The Broadway Musical.* They were intrigued by the possibility of finding an interesting angle on the superhero, and also wanted to create a show that had the chance of being popular on a mass scale. It had been more than 15 years since their last attempt, *A Clockwork Orange,* and they were willing to give the stage another try. Edge also used his free time to scout out and buy, for $15 million, a 120-acre property in Malibu, California. It was located in a canyon that boasted a cottage and a creek rather than on prime oceanfront property. He was later honored by the New York Food Bank, with President Bill Clinton presenting him with the award and Elvis Costello performing an acoustic version of "Where the Streets Have No Name."

When the popular TV program *American Idol* ran a special, two-night "Idol Gives Back" charity show in April, it raised more than $60 million. Bono appeared to promote the ONE charity, and spoke with the contestants about how his trip with Ali to Ethiopia in 1986 had inspired him to give something back. Bono then joined David Bowie to support Lou Reed, who was being honored by his alma mater, Syracuse University. Bono joked that Reed deserved royalties for a lot of U2 songs as one of the band's original inspirations. Edge also received an honorary degree from Boston's Berklee College of Music and quoted AC/DC, "For those about to rock, we salute you!"[9] In May, the band got together to perform a brief set at the Cannes Film Festival to promote *U2 3D,* their new, three-dimensional concert film.

Back in Dublin, Bono and Edge made another application to redevelop the city's historic Temple Bar district and expand their Clarence Hotel. The plans were to involve the demolition of all but the riverside facades of the Clarence Hotel and five neighboring properties they were negotiating to buy. In their place would be built a $163 million, nine-story complex, designed by Norman Foster and topped by a glazed bar with a 360-degree panoramic view of Dublin. U2 finally received permission from the city for the revamp of the hotel, outraging local environmentalists and conservationists who wanted to preserve the classic architecture of the city.

At the end of May, U2 journeyed to Fez, Morocco, to write some new songs with Brian Eno and Daniel Lanois at a traditional riad. The band was last in Fez in 1991 for the "Mysterious Ways" video and had fallen in love with the city's vibe. Larry told U2.com, "It's the first time we've worked with Brian and Dan in a purely songwriting capacity. So it's very different, quite experimental and kind of liberating because of that."[10]

The collaboration began in France a few months earlier with everyone agreeing that location played a big role in influencing the songs. Writing was coming easier to Bono, and the relaxed flow of the sessions was proving to be very beneficial. The group turned up at Fez's Jamai Palace to attend a concert by Iranian singer Parissa and the Dastan Ensemble, who performed poems by Rumi. While in Fez,

U2 recorded with an oud player and some Gnawa and Sufi musicians and finished 10 basic tracks. Bono said:

> I wait for the music to tell me what I'm going to sing. I improvise a lot, and I don't really know where we're going. It's only later that I sit down to write. It's sort of like we're on pilgrimage, barefoot, and we truly don't know where the music will take us.[11]

Bono was especially interested in the Sufi tradition. Eno had referred to this music as "teleological," in contrast to the cyclical nature of African music, on which much of rock is based. Eno was always interested in Arabic music and had been predicting for years that it would create the next fusion. He said:

> There are things I like a lot about Arabic music which are different to what we do in western music and so we have started trying to incorporate some of those elements. It is not a question of sounds so much but of different structural decisions about how things are made.[12]

During their time in Fez, a consensus was emerging about a direction for the new album. Their last two were basic rock records centered around the four band members, but this time they wanted to create something more expansive—they weren't interested in chasing trends, but chasing their muse.

After they left Morocco, Bono attended the TEDGlobal 2007 conference in Tanzania and was criticized for his relentless focus on aid for Africa and neglect of Africa's entrepreneurial culture. He and Bob Geldof then attended the G8 Summit in Heiligendamm, Germany, but as the conference ended the pair denounced world leaders for producing a "deliberately misleading" pledge to fight AIDS and other killer diseases. Bono said he was "exasperated" and called their communiqué "deliberately misleading." The G8 leaders had announced a $60 billion pledge to fight AIDS, malaria, and tuberculosis with great fanfare, but Bono and Geldof were disappointed that they failed to set a timetable and that it contained little new money.

To support efforts to halt the ongoing genocide in Sudan's Darfur region, U2 contributed a cover of John Lennon's "Instant Karma" to *Instant Karma: Amnesty International's Campaign to Save Darfur.* In

July, Bono edited a special edition of *Vanity Fair* devoted to Africa that included on its cover George Clooney, Jay Z, and a new candidate for the U.S. presidency, Barack Obama. Not long after, U2's friend Luciano Pavarotti died of pancreatic cancer at age 71. Bono wrote a tribute:

> Some can sing opera; Luciano Pavarotti was an opera. He lived the songs, his opera was a great mash of joy and sadness; surreal and earthy at the same time; a great volcano of a man who sang fire but spilled over with a love of life in all its complexity, a great and generous friend.[13]

The following month, Bono made a cameo appearance as a shaman called Dr. Robert—his first acting role—in the Beatles' inspired film, *Across the Universe.* He also sang versions of "I Am the Walrus" and "Lucy in the Sky with Diamonds" with Edge and the Secret Machines for the soundtrack.

In September, former President George H. W. Bush awarded Bono the Liberty Medal for his humanitarian work in Africa. It was a bizarre meeting of two men who had been on opposite ends of a parody during the Zoo TV tour. Bono took the chance to address the issue of torture:

> Today I read in the Economist an article reporting that over 38 percent of Americans support some type of torture in exceptional circumstances. My country? No. Your country? Tell me no. Today, when you pin this great honor on me, I ask you, I implore you as an Irishman who has seen some of these things close up, I ask you to remember, you do not have to become a monster to defeat a monster. Your America's better than that.[14]

Bono's position was consistent with his ideals. U2 had been endorsing Amnesty International's position against torture publicly for over 20 years. The fact that Bono found himself receiving a humanitarian award from the father of George W. Bush, the president whose administration had been accused of implementing torture, was rife with irony.

When Anthony DeCurtis interviewed him for *Rolling Stone's* 40-year anniversary issue, Bono referred to living in a "fractional present:"

Now sometimes when I'm walking down the street, and I see a hippie, a punk and so on, I think, "This is exactly this world I pictured when I was a kid." It's like every age is present in this moment. I don't know what it means, exactly. I don't think it's negative or positive. It's just, we do live in a fractional present. No one mood predominates.[15]

This also revealed Bono's ability to effortlessly mash his role as a rock celebrity together with that of a politician, diplomat, and entrepreneur. Bono has never allowed himself to be controlled by only "one mood," and this has given him the freedom to appear with George H. W. Bush one day and Billie Joe Armstrong, the composer of *American Idiot,* the next. It has also led to Bono coming close to winning a Nobel Prize. In December, when a group of Nobel peace laureates awarded him the annual "Man of Peace" prize in recognition of two decades of global antipoverty activism, he said it would be the closest a rock star would come to winning the actual prize. Whether that's true still remains to be seen.

In November, a remastered version of *The Joshua Tree* was released, along with B-sides and outtakes. Bono and Edge played a surprise four-song set at London's Union Chapel to promote it. One of the songs, "Wave of Sorrow," was singled out as an overlooked gem from the sessions and the pair reworked it for the performance. Bono explained that it had originated from his experiences in Ethiopia, where he and Ali volunteered during the famine in 1986. The lyric makes reference to the Queen of Sheba and Emperor Menelik, and contrasts the abundance of the past with the parched famine he witnessed in the 1980s.

Soon after, U2 joined Irish musicians Sinead O'Connor, Christy Moore, and Shane McGowan for a tribute song, "The Ballad of Ronnie Drew." The Dubliner had been suffering from cancer, and proceeds from the song went to the Irish Cancer Society. U2 and the "Dubs" went back to the early 1980s when they would frequently cross paths while on tour, and in 1987 U2 performed the traditional "Springhill Mining Disaster" as a tribute to the band on RTÉ's *The Late Show.* In 1999, Bono had also contributed to a biographical film on Luke Kelly, the Dubliners' lead singer who died in 1984.

In February 2008, U2 was back in the studio with Eno and Lanois, and in May they moved to the south of France to continue the recording. During their time in the south of France, the band became friendly with the son of French rocker Johnny Hallyday. When it came time for Hallyday to release *Le Couer d'Un Homme* (The Heart of a Man), his new album of roots-inspired music, Bono offered him the lyrics to the song, "I Am the Blues," which included the line, "All we do is hurt and break and bruise/I am the blues."[16]

Paul has usually succeeded in avoiding the spotlight, but at Hong Kong's Music Matters conference he caused a stir by lashing out at Internet service providers (ISPs) and harshly criticizing Internet users who downloaded music illegally. He also suggested Radiohead's 2007 *In Rainbows* pay-what-you-want experiment had backfired. Bono later issued an apology to Radiohead, saying:

> We disagree with Paul's assessment of Radiohead's release as "having backfired to a certain extent." We think they were coura- geous and imaginative in trying to figure out some new relation- ship with their audience. Such imagination and courage are in short supply right now . . . they're a sacred talent and we feel blessed to be around at the same time.[17]

Pressure was building on the band to set a release date for the new album. In June, Paul announced it would be coming in October. As work on it intensified, U2 had to give up some commitments and pulled out of Nelson Mandela's 90th birthday party in London, opt- ing to record a video message instead. In July, U2's first three albums—*Boy, October,* and *War*—were re-released with Edge oversee- ing the project. Bono left an online comment on *Rolling Stone*'s Web site about David Fricke's 4.5 star review. He lauded everyone from *New York Times* critic Jon Pareles to old adversaries, Echo and the Bunnymen:

> . . . you can have everything the songs, the production, the face, the attitude but still not have "IT" . . . U2 had nothing really, nothing but "IT" . . . For us music was a sacrament . . . I'm proud of this lit- tle Polaroid of a life I can't fully recall. I miss my boyhood.[18]

In August, portions of the new album leaked on the Net when a passerby used his cell phone to record Bono singing from his villa in Eze. The quality was so bad no one was too concerned, but versions of the "Get on Your Boots" riff still popped up on YouTube. The fol- lowing month, the band realized they would have to change the release date from late 2008 to early 2009—they needed more time to

get the music right. Bono described the new material as being similar in spirit to the transition that led U2 to *Achtung Baby.*[19] By the end
of November, the new album was still unfinished and U2 was in London mixing and rushing around putting the finishing touches on it.
Edge told *Mojo* magazine that the Rick Rubin recordings had been
set aside when they realized his style clashed with U2's approach. It
was déjà vu all over again. He then confirmed that Eno and Lanois
would receive songwriting credits along with the rest of the band.
This was a huge development and the first time in U2's career when
an entire album was to include credited collaborations. Edge added
that the track "Moment of Surrender" was very twenty-first century,
and singled out "Unknown Caller" as a favorite. He also revealed that
they used Death By Audio's Supersonic Fuzz Gun on the song "No
Line on the Horizon," citing the influence of Ben Curtis, the former
Secret Machines' guitarist.[20] A few weeks later, Bono expressed his
satisfaction with *No Line On The Horizon,* the new album's title, listing his favorite song as "Moment of Surrender." He mentioned that
the first single, "Get on Your Boots," was 150 beats per minute, the
fastest song they had ever recorded.[21]

The United States made history in November 2008 by electing
its first president of African American descent, Barack Obama.
Obama's campaign had chosen "City of Blinding Lights" as their
theme song, using it to launch his candidacy in February 2007 and
playing it in Denver at the Democratic Party's national convention in
August 2008. When U2 appeared at the *We Are One* concert held for
President Obama's inauguration, they performed "City of Blinding
Lights" and "Pride" at an open-air concert at the Lincoln Memorial
with a host of acts including Bruce Springsteen and Beyonce.[22]

In the week before *No Line on the Horizon*'s official release, U2
appeared on the BBC performing a live broadcast on Radio 1 and an
"impromptu" gig on top of London's Bush House in homage to the
Beatles' 1969 rooftop concert. They then played "Get on Your Boots"
both at the Grammys and, a week later, at the Brit awards. Each time
the new song was greeted with arched eyebrows and mixed reviews.
When it was released as a single on February 16 it peaked at number
37 in the United States and at number 12 in the United Kingdom,
U2's worst chart showing since "If God Will Send His Angels" in
1997. *Los Angeles Times* music critic, Ann Powers, wrote:

"GOYB" is sharper-edged than "Mysterious Ways," faster than
"Elevation" and more non-linear than "Vertigo." It's dance-rock

with a few small, tricky changes: a very Enoesque bridge to nowhere . . . This is U2's celebratory announcement of a new historical moment, one in which America and the world confront the catastrophes of the recent past and bust out some elbow grease to make things better.[23]

At the end of February, just before the album's official release date, protesters demonstrated outside Ireland's Department of Finance against U2's decision to move their royalties to the Netherlands. The protest was organized by the Debt and Development Coalition Ireland, which campaigns on issues related to the developing world and includes such organizations as Concern Worldwide, Trócaire, Oxfam, and various Catholic missionary orders.[24] Bono was stung by the criticism and responded by saying:

I can understand how people outside the country wouldn't understand how Ireland got to its prosperity but everybody in Ireland knows that there are some very clever people in the Government and in the Revenue who created a financial architecture that prospered the entire nation—it was a way of attracting people to this country who wouldn't normally do business here. What's actually hypocritical is the idea that then you couldn't use a financial services centre in Holland. The real question people need to ask about Ireland's tax policy is: 'Was the nation a net gain benefactor?' And of course it was—hugely so.[25]

On February 27, U2's twelfth studio album, *No Line on the Horizon*, was released in five different formats: a standard jewel case, a vinyl LP, a digipak, a magazine format, and a box format. It debuted at number one in 30 countries and was the band's seventh number-one album in the United States, placing them third behind the Beatles and the Rolling Stones. The album received mixed reviews with *New Musical Express (NME)* giving it 7 out of 10 and calling it "a grand, sweeping, brave record that, while not quite the reinvention they pegged it as, suggests they've got the chops to retain their relevance well into their fourth decade as a band."[26] *Rolling Stone* gave it 5 out of 5, declaring it was their best since *Achtung Baby*, whereas *Pitchfork* gave it only 4.2 out 10, dismissing it as a "pitiful" and "defensive gesture."[27, 28] In a sign of the times, the *Village Voice* wrote, "Like General Motors, a new U2 album is too big to fail" and panned it as "mediocre."[29]

The cover, a white and charcoal-like photograph of Lake Constance, located in Germany, Switzerland, and Austria near the base of the Alps, was taken by Japanese photographer Hiroshi Sugimoto. After it was released, Taylor Deupree, an electronic musician and multimedia artist, blasted the band for ripping off the cover of his 2006 album, *Specification. Fifteen,* which had used an almost identical image.[30]

While much of *No Line on the Horizon* has a sweeping and expansive sound, it suffers from an undertow of scrambled intentions belying its scattered history. Rather than the pocket-rocket pithiness of *How to Dismantle an Atomic Bomb, No Line on the Horizon*'s 11 songs sprawl through long instrumental breaks and shun its predecessor's big hooks. Bono seemed to recognize this, telling *Rolling Stone* that Eno "would listen to '(I Can't Get No) Satisfaction' and say, 'I love that song, but can we get rid of the guitar bits? You know, the part that goes duhnt-duhnt-dunna dun?'"[31]

No Line on the Horizon opens the album with Edge's smearing, Fuzz-Gun-processed guitar and Bono's scarred vocals emerging from the mix. Produced and written with Eno and Lanois, it is the first sign that U2 is reaching for a more sophisticated arrangement since *Pop's* "Discothèque." The album's strongest track is the 7minute 45 second epic, "Moment of Surrender." Using lyrics from at least three years before, the song quickly became a fan favorite, drawing comparisons to "Bad" and "One." Bono beseeches love "to believe in me" as Eno, Lanois, and Edge join on harmonies, lifting the song into the spheres for "a vision over visibility."

The Black Eyed Peas' Will.i.am collaborated with Steve Lillywhite to produce "I'll Go Crazy If I Don't Go Crazy Tonight." It's one of two songs on the album built specifically with middle-of-the-road radio in mind, the other being "Get on Your Boots," which reaches for the hip hooks of *Vertigo,* but falls apart under the weight of forced intentions. One of the albums' standouts, "White As Snow," includes a melody based on the twelfth-century hymn, "Oh Come, Oh Come, Emmanuel," and evokes the thoughts of a soldier dying from a roadside bomb in Afghanistan.[32] The album closes with "Cedars of Lebanon," another lyric sung in character, this time as a foreign correspondent stuck in "this shitty world" where the scent of a rose sometimes "lingers and then it just goes."

Immediately following the release, U2 embarked on a worldwide promotional juggernaut that began with a five-night residency on the *David Letterman Show* during the first week of March. U2 also performed a free morning concert at Fordham University in the Bronx that was broadcast live on *Good Morning America*. In March, Paul announced the new U2 360° stadium tour would begin in the fall of 2009 with a mammoth stage set nicknamed "the Claw" designed by Willie Williams. Sponsored by BlackBerry, it broke U2's prior relationship with Apple. As worldwide CD sales continued to decline, expectations were high that the tour would be U2's major profit maker. The design was intended to make the stage visible from all sides. It didn't have a front or back and was open on the sides, creating a theater-in-the-round experience.

With the new album out and the promotional tour in full swing, Bono revealed that U2 is already planning a follow-up for 2010. He told *Rolling Stone* that the album *Songs of Ascent* would be mellower than the current album, saying, "We're making a kind of heartbreaker, a meditative, reflective piece of work, but not indulgent." He likened it to jazz legend John Coltrane's 1964 classic, "A Love Supreme," and added that the first single would be "Every Breaking Wave," a leftover from *No Line on the Horizon*.[33] While the band was recording in Fez they admitted to being influenced by the Sufi tradition, and *Songs of Ascent* will likely reflect Bono's love for the poetry of Rumi.

On June 30 U2 took to the stage in Barcelona opening their 360° tour to the strains of David Bowie's "Space Oddity" in front of approximately 90,000 cheering fans. The band opened with "Breathe" and closed with "Moment of Surrender." In between they linked up with the International Space Station and played a video message from Desmond Tutu about the ONE campaign. Bono also dedicated "Angel of Harlem" to Michael Jackson, who had died only a few days before, while the band segued into Jackson's "Man in the Mirror" and "Don't Stop 'til You Get Enough."

U2's commitment to human rights was as strong as ever. Before the tour kicked off, the band posted a mask of Aung San Suu Kyi on their website and asked fans to download it and wear it to the concert to show their support for the pro-democracy Nobel Laureate. In Barcelona and later in Milan the band dedicated "Sunday, Bloody Sunday" to the people of Iran who had just endured a violent crackdown after a closely contested election. The entire stage was flooded in green light in support of opposition candidate Mir Hossein Mousavi as Persian text translated as "Listen! Listen! Listen!" rolled across the video screen. The words were from a poem by Jalaladdin Rumi, "The Song of the Reed Flute" which reads in part:

Listen to the reeds as they sway apart,
hear them speak of lost friends . . .
its song and its word break the veil. . . .[34]

CONCLUSION

U2 in 2009 appears remarkably the same, aside from a few wrinkles, grey hairs and receding hairlines, as they did when they burst on the international scene in 1980. Bono, Edge, Adam, Larry, and manager Paul have collectively weathered the past 30-plus years intact, and created music that stands with the greatest of the rock 'n' roll era. They still refuse to be the fools who play it cool in their pursuit of changing the world. In 1981 Bono sang, "I can't change the world, but I can change the world in me." In his press tours he has often repeated a quote he originally made in 2004, "The world is more malleable than you think and it's waiting for you to hammer it into shape."[35] The new songs on *No Line on the Horizon* continue to embody this same spirit to create, in the words of scripture, "on earth as it is in heaven."

As their popularity has grown, so too has their economic and political clout. Like any successful franchise, they have navigated the treacherous waters of public opinion with skill and integrity. In the end, whether U2 likes it or not, their music has become indistinguishable from their political charity work. As U2 faces the future, one of the biggest challenges confronting them is how they will continue to balance the increasing demands of Bono's schedule with being a rock band. Another question is how U2 will adapt to changes in the music industry brought on by the decline of CD sales. Will they put "vision over visibility" or "become a monster to defeat a monster"?

NOTES

1. "Transcript of Bono's Effing NME Award Speech." February 26, 2006. www.u2log.com: http://u2log.com/2006/02/26/transcript-of-bonos-effing-nme-award-speech/ (accessed April 29, 2009).
2. "U2 Is Giving a Voice in Concert with ESPN's Coverage." June 8, 2006. www.nytimes.com: http://query.nytimes.com/gst/fullpage.html?res=9 C06E1DC1531F93BA35755C0A9609C8B63 (accessed April 29, 2009).

3. "For U2, Live Nation Deal Rocks." December 18, 2008. www.wsj.com: http://online.wsj.com/article/SB122956194661216635.html (accessed April 29, 2009).
4. Matt McGee. *U2: A Diary*, 315.
5. "Tour Puts Bono to the Test." November 03, 2006. www.atu2.com/: http://www.atu2.com/news/article.src?ID=4429&Key=&Year=2006&Cat (accessed April 29, 2009).
6. "PM Rejects Bono's Advances." November 08, 2006. www.atu2.com: http://www.atu2.com/news/article.src?ID=4441&Key=&Year=2006&Cat (accessed April 29, 2009).
7. "Costly Red Campaign Reaps Meager $18 Million." March 05, 2007. www.atu2.com: http://www.atu2.com/news/article.src?ID=4578 (accessed April 29, 2009).
8. "A Time for Miracles." March 22, 2007. www.time.com: http://www.time.com/time/magazine/article/0,9171,1601932,00.html (accessed April 29, 2009).
9. McGee, 326.
10. "Songwriting in Morocco, Pt. 1." June 16, 2007. www.atu2.com: http://www.atu2.com/news/article.src?ID=4689&Key=&Year=2007&Cat (accessed April 29, 2009).
11. "Exclusive: Bono's Pilgrimage." June 18, 2007. www.atu2.com: http://www.atu2.com/news/article.src?ID=4674&Key=&Year=2007&Cat (accessed April 29, 2009).
12. "Songwriting in Morocco, Pt. 2." June 20, 2007. www.atu2.com: http://www.atu2.com/news/article.src?ID=4689&Key=&Year=2007&Cat (accessed April 29, 2009).
13. "Bono's tribute to Pavarotti." September 6, 2007. news.bbc.co.uk: http://news.bbc.co.uk/2/hi/entertainment/6981703.stm (accessed September 6, 2007).
14. "Bono & DATA." September 27, 2007. www.constitutioncenter.org/libertymedal: http://www.constitutioncenter.org/libertymedal/recipient_2007.html (accessed April 29, 2009).
15. "The U2 frontman sits down for our 40th anniversary to talk about the future, the Buzzcocks and reasons to compromise." October 31, 2007. www.atu2.com: http://www.atu2.com/news/article.src?ID=4785&Key=&Year=2007&Cat (accessed April 29, 2009).
16. "I Am The Blues." www.mp3lyrics.org: http://www.mp3lyrics.org/j/johnny-hallyday/i-am-the-blues (accessed April 29, 2009).
17. "U2 defends Radiohead in letter to *NME* Magazine." June 25, 2008. www.atu2.com: http://www.atu2.com/news/article.src?ID=5023&Key=&Year=2008&Cat (accessed April 29, 2009).
18. "Exclusive: Bono Remembers U2's *Boy*. August 4, 2008. www.rollingstone.com: http://www.rollingstone.com/rockdaily/index.php/2008/08/04/exclusive-bono-remembers-u2s-boy/ (accessed April 29, 2009).

19. "Next U2 Album Pushed to Early 2009." September 3, 2008. www.atu2.com: http://www.atu2.com/news/article.src?ID=5083&Key =&Year=2008&Cat (accessed April 29, 2009).

20. "U2 Album Still Not Finished." November 24, 2008. www.atu2.com: http://www.atu2.com/news/article.src?ID=5134&Key=&Year=2008& Cat (accessed April 29, 2009).

21. Race-goer Bono's on to another winner as U2 album passes finish line." December 27, 2008. www.atu2.com: http://www.atu2.com/news/article .src?ID=5342&Key=&Year=2008&Cat (accessed April 29, 2009).

22. "U2 'honoured' to be involved with Obama celebrations." January 19, 2009. www.atu2.com: http://www.atu2.com/news/article.src?ID=5328 &Key=&Year=2009&Cat (accessed April 29, 2009).

23. "Snap Judgment: U2's new single, 'Get on Your Boots.'" January 19, 2009. www.latimes.com: http://latimesblogs.latimes.com/music_blog/ 2009/01/snap-judgment-u.html (accessed April 29, 2009).

24. "Protest at U2's tax exile status." February 25, 2009. www.atu2.com: http://www.atu2.com/news/article.src?ID=5366&Key=&Year=2009& Cat (accessed April 29, 2009).

25. "Bono 'hurt' by criticism of U2 move to Netherlands to cut tax." February 27, 2009. www.atu2.com: http://www.atu2.com/news/article .src?ID=5381&Key=&Year=2009&Cat (accessed April 29, 2009).

26. "Album Review: U2's No Line On The Horizon." February 26, 2009. www.nme.com: http://www.nme.com/reviews/u2/10149 (accessed April 29, 2009).

27. "Album Review: U2's No Line On The Horizon." February 29, 2009. www.rollingstone.com: http://www.rollingstone.com/reviews/album/ 26079033/review/26212378/no_line_on_the_horizon (accessed April 29, 2009).

28. "Album Review: U2's No Line On The Horizon." March 2, 2009. www.pitchfork.com: http://pitchfork.com/reviews/albums/12730-no-line-on-the-horizon/ (accessed April 29, 2009).

29. "No U2 Schadenfreude, Baby." March 10, 2009. www.villagevoice.com: http://www.villagevoice.com/2009-03-11/music/no-u2-schadenfreude-baby/ (accessed April 29, 2009).

30. "U2 Talk 'Horizon' Follow Up, Spider-Man Musical in Rolling Stone Cover Story." March 4, 2009. www.rollingstone.com: http://www. rollingstone.com/rockdaily/index.php/2009/03/04/u2-talk-horizon-follow-up-spider-man-musical-in-rolling-stone-cover-story/ (accessed April 29, 2009).

31. "U2 album artwork branded 'rip off.'" January 21, 2009. www.nme.com: http://www.nme.com/news/u2/42195 (accessed April 29, 2009).

32. "White As Snow: U2's most intimate song." February 13, 2009. www.guardian.co.uk: http://www.guardian.co.uk/music/musicblog/ 2009/feb/13/u2-white-as-snow (accessed April 29, 2009).

33. "U2 Talk 'Horizon' Follow Up, Spider-Man Musical in Rolling Stone Cover Story." March 4, 2009. www.rollingstone.com: http://www.rolling stone.com/rockdaily/index.php/2009/03/04/u2-talk-horizon-follow-up-spider-man-musical-in-rolling-stone-cover-story/ (accessed April 29, 2009).
34. "Iran: U2's green-tinted tributes to Iranian protesters." July 10, 2009. http://latimesblogs.latimes.com/babylonbeyond/2009/07/iran-u2-tributes-iranian-protestors.html (accessed September 14, 2009).
35. "Because We Can, We Must." Commencement Address by Bono, co-founder of DATA (Debt AIDS Trade Africa), and lead singer of U2, May 17, 2004. http://www.upenn.edu/almanac/between/2004/commence-b .html (accessed April 29, 2009).

U2's Studio Albums

Boy (October 1980)
Producer: Steve Lillywhite
Track Listing: I Will Follow/Twilight/ An Cat Dubh/Into the Heart/ Out of Control/ Stories for Boys/ The Ocean/ A Day Without Me/ Another Time, Another Place/ The Electric Co./ Shadows and Tall Trees

October (October 1981)
Producer: Steve Lillywhite
Track Listing: Gloria/ I Fall Down/ I Threw a Brick Through a Window/ Rejoice/ Fire/ Tomorrow/ October/ With a Shout/ Stranger in a Strange Land/ Scarlet/ Is That All?

War (March 1983)
Producer: Steve Lillywhite
Track Listing: Sunday Bloody Sunday/ Seconds/ New Year's Day/Like a Song . . . / Drowning Man/ The Refugee/ Two Hearts Beat as One/ Red Light/ Surrender/ "40"

The Unforgettable Fire (October 1984)
Producers: Brian Eno & Daniel Lanois
Track Listing: A Sort of Homecoming/ Pride (In the Name of Love)/Wire/ The Unforgettable Fire/ Promenade/ 4th of July/ Bad/ Indian Summer Sky/ Elvis Presley and America/ MLK

The Joshua Tree (March 1987)
Producers: Daniel Lanois & Brian Eno
Track Listing: Where the Streets Have No Name/ I Still Haven't Found What I'm Looking For/ With or Without You/ Bullet the Blue Sky/ Running to Stand Still/ Red Hill Mining Town/ In God's Country/ Trip Through Your Wires/ One Tree Hill/ Exit/ Mothers of the Disappeared

Rattle and Hum (March 1988)
Producers: Daniel Lanois & Brian Eno
Track Listing: Helter Skelter/ Van Dieman's Land/ Desire/ Hawkmoon 269/ All Along the Watchtower/ I Still Haven't Found What I'm Looking For/ Freedom for My People/ Silver and Gold/ Pride (In the Name of Love)/ Angel of Harlem/ Love Rescue Me/ When Love Comes to Town/ Heartland/ God Part II/ The Star Spangled Banner/ Bullet the Blue Sky/ All I Want Is You

Achtung Baby (November 1991)
Producer: Daniel Lanois with special thanks to Brian Eno
Track Listing: Zoo Station/ Even Better Than the Real Thing/ One/ Until the End of the World/ Who's Gonna Ride Your Wild Horses/ So Cruel/ The Fly/ Mysterious Ways/ Trying to Throw Your Arms Around the World/ Ultraviolet (Light My Way)/ Acrobat/ Love Is Blindness

Zooropa (July 1993)
Producers: Flood, Brian Eno & The Edge
Track Listing: Zooropa/ Babyface/ Numb/ Lemon/ Stay (Faraway, So Close)/ Daddy's Gonna Pay for Your Crashed Car/ Some Days Are Better Than Others/ The First Time/ Dirty Day/ The Wanderer

Pop (March 1997)
Producer: Flood
Track Listing: Discothèque/ Do You Feel Loved/ Mofo/ If God Will Send His Angels/ Staring at the Sun/ Last Night on Earth/ Gone/ Miami/ The Playboy Mansion/ If You Wear That Velvet Dress/ Please/ Wake Up Dead Man

All That You Can't Leave Behind (October 2000)
Producers: Daniel Lanois & Brian Eno
Track Listing: Beautiful Day/ Stuck in a Moment You Can't Get Out Of/ Elevation/ Walk On/ Kite/ In a Little While/ Wild Honey/ Peace on Earth/ When I Look at the World/ New York/ Grace

How to Dismantle an Atomic Bomb (November 2004)
Producer: Steve Lillywhite
Track Listing: Vertigo/ Miracle Love/ Sometimes You Can't Make It on Your Own/ Love and Peace or Else/ City of Blinding Lights/ All Because of You/ A Man and a Woman/ Crumbs from Your Table/ One Step Closer/ Original of the Species/ Yahweh

No Line on the Horizon (2009)
Producers: Daniel Lanois & Brian Eno
Track Listing: No Line on the Horizon/ Magnificent/ Moment of Surren-der/ Unknown Caller/ I'll Go Crazy If I Don't Go Crazy Tonight/ Get on Your Boots/ Stand Up Comedy/ Fez - Being Born/ White As Snow/ Breathe/ Cedars of Lebanon

U2's Number 1 Singles

(UK)

1988: "Desire"
1991: "The Fly"
1997: "Discothèque"
2000: "Beautiful Day"
2004: "Vertigo"
2005: "Sometimes You Can't Make It on Your Own"

(US)

1987: "With or Without You"
"I Still Haven't Found What I'm Looking For"

U2's Videos

1980: "I Will Follow"

1981: "Gloria"

1982: "A Celebration"

1983: "New Year's Day"
"Two Hearts Beat as One"
"Sunday Bloody Sunday" (live)

1984: "Pride (In the Name of Love)"
"The Unforgettable Fire"
"A Sort of Homecoming"

1985: "Bad" (live)

1987: "With or Without You"
"I Still Haven't Found What I'm Looking For"
"Where the Streets Have No Name"
"Red Hill Mining Town"
"Spanish Eyes"
"In God's Country"
"One Tree Hill"

"Christmas (Baby, Please Come Home)"

1988: "Desire"
"Angel of Harlem"

1989: "When Love Comes to Town"
"All I Want Is You"

1990: "Night and Day"

1991: "The Fly"
"Mysterious Ways"
"One"

1992: "Even Better Than the Real Thing"
"Until the End of the World"
"Who's Gonna Ride Your Wild Horses"

1993: "Love Is Blindness"
"Numb"
"Lemon"
"Stay (Faraway, So Close!)"
"I've Got You Under My Skin" (with Frank Sinatra)

1995: "Miss Sarajevo"
"Hold Me, Thrill Me, Kiss Me, Kill Me"

1997: "Discothèque"
"Staring at the Sun"
"Last Night on Earth"
"Please"
"If God Will Send His Angels"
"Mofo"

1998: "The Sweetest Thing"

2000: "The Ground Beneath Her Feet"
"Beautiful Day"

2001: "Stuck in a Moment You Can't Get Out Of"
"Walk On"
"Elevation"

2002: "Electrical Storm"

2003: "The Hands That Built America"

2004: "Vertigo"
"All Because of You"

2005: "Sometimes You Can't Make It on Your Own"
"City of Blinding Lights"
"Original of the Species"

2006: "One" (with Mary J. Blige)
"The Saints Are Coming" (with Green Day)
"Window in the Skies"

2008: "I Believe in Father Christmas"

2009: "Get on Your Boots"
"Magnificent"

U2's Awards

Grammy Awards (22 Awards)

1988:   Album of the Year: *The Joshua Tree*
           Best Rock Duo or Group with Vocal: *The Joshua Tree*

1989:   Best Rock Duo or Group with Vocal: "Desire"
           Best Performance Music Video: "Where the Streets Have No Name"

1993:   Best Rock Duo or Group with Vocal: *Achtung Baby*

1994:   Best Alternative Music Album: *Zooropa*

1995:   Best Long Form Music Video: *Zoo TV: Live from Sydney*

2001:   Best Rock Duo or Group with Vocal, Song of the Year, Record of the Year: "Beautiful Day"

2002:   Best Rock Album: *All That You Can't Leave Behind*
           Best Rock Duo or Group with Vocal: "Elevation"
           Best Pop Duo or Group with Vocal: "Stuck in a Moment You Can't Get Out Of"
           Record of the Year: "Walk On"

2005:   Best Short Form Music Video, Best Rock Song, Best Rock Duo or Group with Vocal: "Vertigo"

2006:   Album of the Year: *How to Dismantle an Atomic Bomb*
           Song of the Year: "Sometimes You Can't Make It on Your Own"
           Best Rock Duo or Group with Vocal, Best Rock Song: "City of Blinding Lights"
           Best Rock Album: *How to Dismantle an Atomic Bomb*

The BRIT Awards (7 Awards)

1983: Best Live Act (discretionary award)
1988: Best International Group
1989: Best International Group
1990: Best International Group
1992: Best International Group
1998: Best International Group
2001: Best International Group
Outstanding Contribution to Music

Further Reading

U2 Web Sites

http://www.u2.com/
http://www.atu2.com
http://scatterolight.blogspot.com/
http://www.threechordsandthetruth.net/
http://www.u2faqs.com/
http://www.u2tours.com/
http://www.u2wanderer.org/
http://www.u2newzooland.com/
http://u2log.com/
http://u2tour.de/
http://interference.com/
http://www.u2place.com/
http://www.u2gigs.com/
http://www.u2setlists.com/
http://www.u2star.com/blog/
http://u2station.com/
http://u2achtung.com/
http://u2_interviews.tripod.com/index.html
http://u2info.com/

U2 Books

Alan, Carter. *Outside Is America: U2 in the US.* (Boston: Faber and Faber, 1992).

Assayas, Michka. *Bono On Bono.* (London: Hodder & Stoughton Ltd., 2005).

Cogan, Visnja. *U2: An Irish Phenomenon.* (Cork: The Collins Press, 2006).

Flanagan, Bill. *U2 At the End of the World.* (London: Bantam Press, 1995).

Friday, Gavin. *The Light and Dark.* (Utrecht, Von B Press, 1991).

Graham, Bill. *U2 The Early Days: Another Time, Another Place.* (London: Octopus Publishing Group, 1989).

McCormick, Neil. *Killing Bono.* (New York, Pocket Books, 2004).

McGee, Matt. *U2: A Diary.* (London: Omnibus Press, 2008).

Negativland. *Fair Use—The Story Of The Letter U And The Numeral 2.* (Concord, CA, Seeland, 1995).

Rolling Stone. *U2: The Ultimate Compendium of Interviews, Articles, Facts and Opinions.* (New York: Hyperion, 1994).

Stokes, Niall. *U2: Into the Heart.* (London: Carlton Books, 2005).

U2 by U2. (New York: HarperCollins, 2006).

Waters, John. *Race Of Angels—The Genesis Of U2.* (London, Fourth Estate, 1994).

Index

Pay-what-want experiment, 136
"Peace on Earth" (U2), 102, 107
Pearl Jam, 122, 130
Pearlman, Sandy, 29
Peltier, Leonard, 117
Peters, Mike, 35
Petro, Christina, 80
PiL, 17, 36
Pitchfork (magazine), 138
Plank, Conny, 41
Platinum records, 50
"The Playboy Mansion" (U2), 93
Poetry, 31, 44, 60, 77, 84, 132
Pogues, 59, 127
Police, 54
Politics
  Bono on, 36, 39, 102
  The Clash and, 114
  elections, 33, 81, 101, 119, 140
  Geldorf and, 47–48
  Mullen on, 80
  party conventions, 118, 119, 137
  radio and, 30
  War and, 32
  See also King, Martin Luther Jr.;
    specific issues
Pop (U2), 91–94, 98, 117
PopMart tour, 94–98
Porter, Cole, 73, 86
Post Office Workers' Union Band,
  3, 32
Post-punk, 30
Poverty, 118, 123, 130. *See also*
  Debt relief
Premier Talent, 18, 20
Presley, Elvis, 45, 46, 67, 76, 80, 90
Pretenders, 37, 45
"Pride (In The Name Of Love)"
  (U2)
  basics, 35, 40, 45, 47
  Greenpeace album and, 70
  Lanois and, 43
  performances, 51, 62, 63, 118,
    137

Prince, 91
Prine, John, 70
Product (RED), 125, 129, 130–131
Project Art Center performances, 8
Propaganda (magazine), 53, 78, 90
Punk, 5, 6, 7. *See also specific artists
  and bands*

Racism, 82
Radiators From Outer Space, 5, 6
Radio
  beginnings, 11, 18–19
  Bono and, 21
  Eno and, 43
  MOR, 139
  "New Year's Day" and, 35
  Pop and, 92
  Unforgettable Fire and, 50
  US, 20, 25, 30
Radio and Records AOR charts, 35
Radiohead, 84, 136
Raging Bull (film), 70
Ramones, 5, 7, 108
Rattle and Hum (album/film), 58,
  66–67, 68, 69–70, 104
R&B, 58, 63
Rebellion, 2, 6, 10, 31, 34, 58, 78.
  See also
  Conformity/nonconformity
Record Mirror (magazine), 10, 11,
  25
"Red Hill Mining Town" (U2), 61
Red Hot and Blue compilation, 73
Red Rocks (Colorado), 37–38
Reed, Lou, 51, 76, 81, 132
Reggae, 70
Religion
  albums/songs and, 32, 33, 60, 77,
    85, 93, 94, 107, 118, 139,
    141
  Bono and, 84, 85–86, 98, 111,
    118, 131
  festivals, 65
  influences by, 1–2, 19, 31

About the Author

David Kootnikoff is a Canadian writer who
is forever grateful to U2
for providing him with his victorious high school campaign slogan
for Student Council Vice-President in 1984–85:

"I Will Sing a New Song"